The Manhattan Doctor Guide

THE
Manhattan
DOCTOR GUIDE

New York's
Most Talked-About Physicians

Richard D. Topp

RadComm, Inc.
NEW YORK, NY

The Manhattan Doctor Guide

RadComm, Inc.
Box 717
New York, NY 10028
(212) 861-1106
www.HealthQ.com

Copyright © 1998 by RadComm, Inc.

First Printing 1998

Printed in the United States of America

ISBN: 09663834-0-0

10 9 8 7 6 5 4 3 2 1

Cover design, text design, and composition by
John Reinhardt Book Design

Contents

Preface

How do you find a new doctor?
How does everyone find a new doctor?

We ask our friends, our associates, and our mothers. Frequently, we ask our doctors, who in turn find their own doctors by asking their friends and associates. Except for the few who advertise, all referrals to doctors are recommendations: they are all word of mouth. Each of us has a personal network, which we use to help us make important decisions but recent changes in health care delivery may have expanded our choices but not our ability to evaluate these choices.

The Manhattan Doctor Guide was developed to extend our personal networks. The Manhattan Doctor Guide is the only one of its kind: a comprehensive, up-to-date guide to medical care in New York City. Based on a survey of 6,000 people in Manhattan and collected during the spring and summer of 1997, it is guided by the principle that consumers are the best judges of the health care services they receive.

THE SURVEY

The survey contained fifteen consumer-oriented questions divided into five groups: Appointments, Communications, Office Environment, Administration and an Overall Evaluation. All questions were answered anonymously and on a scale of 1–10. For the convenience of the reader, the results have been combined into aggregate scores for each Doctor and Office. The Overall score represents the response to a single, general question. Select patient comments are included to give you the kind of insider information can only be obtained from a sampling of 6,000 respondents. In a few cases no respondent had a comment about a particular doctor, therefore we have left these Patient Comment sections blank. Similarly, in a few cases doctors did not wish to share information about their offices and policies, we have left these entries blank as well.

THE RESULTS ARE IN

We learned a lot from the survey. We learned that 89% of the doctors in our guide are viewed positively by their patients. We learned that 69% of all Manhattan doctors practice on the East Side. We learned that there are doctors offices in NYC where Cambodian, Afrikaans and Tagalog are spoken as well as Spanish, Yiddish and Mandarin.

We learned that patients usually base their evaluations of their doctors on three criteria: Availability, Communication and Competence. The highest scoring doctors were those who made themselves readily available for appointments and telephone calls, communicate sensitively, provide professional care and have staffs that are competent and compassionate

In addition to a doctor's general reputation, assessed by talking to others, patients frequently assess a doctor's competence by considering his or her associations with medical schools and hospitals. Respondents often identified their doctor by saying "she went to Columbia" or " he's at Lenox Hill or NYU or NY Hospital." **The Manhattan Doctor Guide** contains information about the medical school attended and hospital affiliations of the all the doctors listed. All the doctors in this guide are reported to be Board Certified in their principal specialties. Every listed doctor's office was contacted to determine fees and credit card acceptability. We asked each doctor's office to list the major health plans for which it was a provider and have provided an index to help you identify the providers included in your insurance plan.

We also learned that patients are sometimes inconsistent in their evaluations. Occasionally, for example, patients would give their doctor high ratings for availability and then comment "The doctor always keeps me waiting and doesn't provide enough time during appointments." Or respondents might give a doctor poor scores, then comment "my doctor is excellent but has an unbearable staff." As interviewers we were struck by these inconsistencies and have tried to select comments that are consistent with the numeric ratings. This was not always possible while accurately reflecting what the respondents said; therefore some of the Patient Comments may appear to be inconsistent with the scores. We hope that our readers recognize that although we believe that we received honest and accurate appraisals from our respondents; they, like us, are not perfectly consistent.

How do you find a good doctor? The way you always have, through networking and research.

How do you find a good doctor in Manhattan? By using this guide to expand your personal health care network and provide you with most of the information you need to make an informed health care decision.

In an effort to provide better access to the survey data we have indexed the data in many ways. Doctors are listed in alphabetic order in the body of the guide. All indices are in Specialty order and then alphabetic except the Top Five Index where the doctors are listed in descending order. The Insurance Provider Index will help direct the reader to the providers in their plan. If a consulting opinion is required, check with the Specialty and Insurer indexes.

OUR WEB SITE

Additional help and an opportunity to take part in our survey can be found at our Web Site:

HTTP://WWW.HEALTHQ.COM

There you can participate in our survey and find useful, patient-oriented, information about a variety of health topics. You can also participate by sending a self-addressed, stamped envelope to:

The Manhattan Doctor Guide
Box 717
New York, NY 10028

On our Web Site you can check the credentials of any licensed NYS professional, find information about doctors from the AMA and check on information about many diseases and conditions. Our goal is to constantly widen our information gathering and to broaden our coverage in both breadth and depth.

While there is no "perfect" doctor, there is a "perfect" doctor for each of us. In fact, there are many doctors who are perfect or close to perfect for all of us. We remind our readers that neither RadComm, Inc., the author, nor any or its' employees are engaged in the delivery of health care services. It is up to each of us to find the best doctor(s) for ourselves and we hope that this guide offers you some assistance as you make these decisions.

How to Read this Guide

Baiocco, Peter, M.D.	DOCTOR	OFFICE	OVERALL

GASTROENTEROLOGY · INTERNAL MEDICINE

9.0   8.1   9.6

LANGUAGES	MEDICAL SCHOOL	HOSPITAL AFFILIATIONS
French	Mt. Sinai, NY '78	Lenox Hill
Italian		
Spanish		

Peter J. Baiocco, M.D.
1317 Third Ave
734-8811

GENERAL OFFICE INFORMATION

		HMO/PPO
First Visit: _____ $175		Aetna/USH
Regular Visit: __ $100		Blue Choice
Accessible: _____ Yes		Cigna
Interpreters: ____ No		Healthsource
Medicare: _____ Yes		Magna Care
Medicaid: _____ No		Oxford
Evenings: _____ No		PHS/Guardian
Saturdays: _____ No		PHCS
AmEx: _____ Yes		
Visa/MC: _____ No		

PATIENT COMMENTS

His patients say:

he's very attentive and dedi-cated.

Another says:

he's considerate of money. If one prescription costs more than an equivalent one, he'll give you the cheaper one.

The Scores

The DOCTOR score was calculated by averaging the numeric scores from a number of survey questions about each doctor and displaying the results on a scale of 1–10. Similarly, the OFFICE score was calculated by averaging the numeric scores from another group of survey questions about each doctor's office and displaying the results on a scale of 1–10. The OVERALL score represents the average response to a single question requesting an overall impression of each respondent's experience.

The Patient Comments

The PATIENT COMMENTS are examples of what previous patients chose to tell us about their doctors. They are direct quotations and were selected to provide our readers with insight into how the services rendered were perceived by that patient.

Office Information & Prices

The Office Information has been provided by the doctor's offices themselves and is presented to provide you with up-to-date information about office policies, prices and procedures. The prices reflect the doctor's average fees. They do not include tests or other diagnostic procedures which may be required. Many doctors fees vary reflecting the different amounts of complexity and time required for each case. The fee you are charged maybe different than those quoted. In a few cases, doctors did not provide us with the information we requested. We have attempted to complete the necessary information without their cooperation.

Accessibility information and services for the Hearing Impaired information has been gathered from the doctors offices. Indices are provided for both.

HMO/PPO Information

Has been provided by the doctor's offices to enable you to find providers who participate in your health plcan. An Insurance Provider index is provided to assist you in finding doctor's who are providers for your insurance plan.

"Private Practice" indicates that the doctor is not a provider for any HMO or PPO. These doctors charge a fee for their service's which may or may not be covered, wholly or in part, by your insurance.

Indices are provided for Medicare and Medicaid providers.

Language Information

The foreign languages listed for each doctor reflect languages spoken by the doctor or by someone on the doctor's staff. An index is provided to help you find a doctors offices where each language is understood.

Hospital Affiliations, Specialty Information and Medical Education Information

Provided by the doctor's offices, The New York State Medical Directory, The American Medical Association database and various other sources. Indices are provided to help you find doctors affiliated with specific hospitals and specialties.

Top 5 Doctors

Cardiology
Andersen, Holly S. MD
Ellis, George C., MD
Mattes, Leonard, MD
Graf, Jeffrey H, MD
Franklin, Kenneth W, MD

Family Practice
Clements, Jerry, MD
Aguero, Jose, MD
Braun, James F., MD
Buchel, Tamara L., MD
Bauchman, Gail, MD

Gastroenterology
Baiocco, Peter, MD
Altman, Kenneth A., MD
Goldberg, Edward S., MD
Adler, Howard, MD
Cantor, Michael C., MD

Geriatrics
Wiechowski, Michael, MD
Babitz, Lisa E., MD
Schayes, Bernard, MD
Halper, Peter, MD
Levy, Albert, MD

Hematology
Beautyman, Elizabeth J., MD
Lewin, Margaret, MD

Udesky, Robert A., MD
Edwards, Colleen A., MD
Geltman, Richard L., MD

Infectious Diseases
Hart, Catherine, MD
Nash, Thomas W, MD
Fried, Richard P., MD
Bell, Evan T., MD
Wallach, Jeffrey , MD

Internal Medicine
Hart, Catherine, MD
Newman Mark R., MD
Moyer Lawson, MD
Baiocco Peter, MD
Young Kevin S., MD

Medical Oncology
Diamond, Carol, MD
Belenkov, Elliot, MD
Lewin, Margaret, MD
Udesky, Robert A., MD
Geltman, Richard L., MD

OB/GYN
Cavalli, Adele, MD
Livoti, Carol, MD
Berman, Alvin, MD
Sassoon, Albert K., MD, MPH
Zilberstein, Inga, MD

Pediatrics

Stein, Barry B., MD
Skog, Donald R., MD
Smith, David I., MD
Wishnick, Marcia M., MD
Murphy, Ramon J. C., MD

Pulmonology

Nash, Thomas W, MD
Falk, George A., MD

Posner, David H., MD
Konecky, Alan, MD
Schwartz, Lawrence P., MD

Rheumatolgy

Leventhal, Gerald H., MD
Bernstein, Donald H., MD
Kramer, Sara, MD
Radin, Allen, MD
Bernstein, Stephen J., MD

Specialty Index

Adolescent Medicine
Pegler, Cynthia, MD

Allergy & Immunology
Falk, George A., MD
Levine, Susan, MD
Lichtenfeld, Amy D., MD

Cardiology
Andersen, Holly S., MD
Ellis, George C., MD
Franklin, Kenneth W., MD
Graf, Jeffrey H., MD
Kennish, Arthur, MD
Mattes, Leonard, MD
Mueller, Richard L., MD

Critical Care Medicine
Bahr, Gerald S., MD
Konecky, Alan, MD
Posner, David H., MD

Dermatology
Demar, Leon K., MD
Kling, Alan R., MD
Long, Willam T., Dr
Scheiner, Avery M., MD

Emergency Medicine
Isaacs, Daryl M., MD
Lewin, Neal A., MD

Endocrinology
Bernstein, Gerald, MD
Colt, Edward, MD
Merker, Edward, MD
Park, Constance, MD

Family Practice
Aguero, Jose, MD
Bauchman, Gail, MD
Braun, James F., MD
Buchel, Tamara L., MD
Chung, Bruce, MD
Clements, Jerry, MD
Goldberg, Richard, MD
Horowitz, Mark E., MD
Leeds, Gary, MD
Leichman, Gerald, MD
Levy, Albert, MD
Olmscheid, Bruce, MD
Ravetz, Valerie, MD
Shepard, Richard, MD
Tamarin, Steven, MD

Gastroenterology
Adler, Howard, MD
Altman, Kenneth A., MD
Arons, Elliot, MD
Attia, Albert, MD
Baiocco, Peter, MD
Bearnot, Robert, MD
Brettholz, Edward, MD

Gastroenterology (cont'd)

Cantor, Michael C., MD
Dubin, Richard, MD
Goldberg, Edward S., MD
Harris, Lucinda A., MD
Loria, Jeffrey M., MD
Lustbader, Ian, MD
Pearlman, Kenneth I., MD
Present, Daniel H., MD
Weber, Scott, MD
Weintraub, Gerald, MD
Yaffe, Bruce H., MD
Zachary, Kirk J., MD

General Practice

Shapiro, Irene, MD

General Surgery

Cho, Sam K., MD

Geriatrics

Babitz, Lisa E., MD
Bernstein, Donald H., MD
Goodman, Karl, MD
Halper, Peter, MD
Kamlet, David A., MD
Levy, Albert, MD
Mernick, Mitchel, MD
Schayes, Bernard, MD
Wiechowski, Michael, MD

Gynecology

Beitner, Orit, MD
Berman, Joan K., MD
Fishbane-Mayer, Jill, MD
Hirsch, Lissa, MD

Hematology

Beautyman, Elizabeth J., MD
Buckner, Jeffrey A., MD
Edwards, Colleen A., MD
Frankel, Etta B., MD
Geltman, Richard L., MD

Lewin, Margaret, MD
Udesky, Robert A.., MD
Vizel-Schwartz, Monique, MD

Infectious Diseases

Bell, Evan T., MD
Fisher, Laura, MD
Fried, Richard P., MD
Gale, Robert K., MD
Hart, Catherine, MD
Levine, Susan, MD
Montana, John, MD
Nash, Thomas W., MD
Rudin, Debra, MD
Silverman, David, MD
Wallach, Jeffrey, MD

Internal Medicine

Abrams, Robert S., MD
Adler, Howard, MD
Adler, Jack J., MD
Adler, Mitchell A., MD
Altman, Kenneth A., MD
Ament, Joseph D., MD
Amiraian, Richard H., MD
Andersen, Holly S., MD
Arons, Elliot, MD
Attia, Albert, MD
Babitz, Lisa E., MD
Bahr, Gerald S., MD
Baiocco, Peter, MD
Bardes, Charles L., MD
Barnes, Edward, MD
Baskin, David H., MD
Bearnot, Robert, MD
Beautyman, Elizabeth J., MD
Beitler, Martin, MD
Belenkov, Elliot, MD
Bell, Evan T., MD
Bendo, Dominick, MD
Bernstein, Donald H., MD
Bernstein, Gerald, MD
Bernstein, Stephen J., MD

Blye, Ellen, MD

Brandon, Donald E., MD

Bregman, Zachary, MD

Brettholz, Edward, MD

Bruno, Peter J., MD

Buckner, Jeffrey A., MD

Burns, Margaret M., MD

Cantor, Michael C., MD

Charap, Peter, MD

Cohen, Albert, MD

Cohen, Robert L., MD

Colt, Edward, MD

De Cotis, Sue Gene, MD

Dellosso, John, MD

Dhalla, Satish, MD

Diamond, Carol, MD

Drapkin, Arnold, MD

Dubin, Richard, MD

Edwards, Colleen A., MD

Ellis, George C., MD

Falk, George A., MD

Fallick, Nina, MD

Fisher, Laura, MD

Frankel, Etta B., MD

Franklin, Kenneth W., MD

Fried, Richard P., MD

Friedman, Jeffrey P., MD

Furman, Alice, MD

Gale, Robert K., MD

Geltman, Richard L., MD

Glick, Jeffrey, MD

Goldberg, Edward S., MD

Golden, Flavia A., MD

Goodman, Karl, MD

Graf, Jeffrey H., MD

Grossman, Howard A., MD

Halper, Peter, MD

Hammer, David, MD

Harris, Lucinda A., MD

Hart, Catherine, MD

Hauptman, Allen S., MD

Higgins, Lawrence A., DO, MPH

Horbar, Gary, MD

Horovitz, H. Leonard, MD

Hurd Beverly, MD

Isaacs, Daryl M, MD

Kabakow, Bernard, MD

Kadet, Alan, MD

Kamlet, David A., MD

Kaufman, David L., MD

Keller, Raymond S., MD

Kennedy, James T., MD

Kennish, Arthur, MD

Klein, Susan, MD

Konecky, Alan, MD

Kramer, Sara, MD

Lamm, Steven, MD

Langelier, Carolyn A., MD

Larson, Carol, MD

Leventhal, Gerald H., MD

Levine, Susan, MD

Lewin, Margaret, MD

Lewin, Neal A., MD

Lichtenfeld, Amy D., MD

Loria, Jeffrey M., MD

Lustbader, Ian, MD

Lutsky, Eric, MD

Mattes, Leonard, MD

Mellow, Nancy L., MD

Merker, Edward, MD

Mernick, Mitchel, MD

Montana, John, MD

Moyer, Lawson, MD

Mueller, Richard L., MD

Nadel, Lester, MD

Nash, Thomas W., MD

Newman, Mark R., MD

Nicolaides, Maria N., MD

Painter, Lucy N., MD

Palumbo, Michael J., MD

Park, Constance, MD

Pearlman, Kenneth I., MD

Perskin, Michael, MD

Pitaro, Gregory, MD

Posner, David H., MD

Present, Daniel H., MD

Internal Medicine (cont'd)

Radin, Allen, MD
Rodman, John S., MD
Rooney, Ellen, MD
Ruden, Ronald, MD
Rudin, Debra, MD
Schayes, Bernard, MD
Schwartz, Lawrence P., MD
Shay, William E., MD
Silverman, David, MD
Solomon, David Y., MD
Sorra, Lembitu, MD
Strauss, Steven, MD
Suozzi, William, MD
Udesky, Robert A., MD
Underberg, James A., MD
Vizel-Schwartz, Monique, MD
Wallach, Jeffrey, MD
Weber, Scott, MD
Weiner, David J., MD
Weinstein, Melvin, MD
Weintraub, Gerald, MD
Weiser, Frank M., MD
Weiss, Nancy L., MD
Wiechowski, Michael, MD
Woronoff, Richard S., MD
Yaffe, Bruce H., MD
Yanoff, Allen, MD
Young, Kevin S., MD
Zachary, Kirk J., MD

Medical Oncology

Belenkov, Elliot, MD
Buckner, Jeffrey A., MD
Diamond, Carol, MD
Frankel, Etta B., MD
Geltman, Richard L., MD
Kabakow, Bernard, MD
Lewin, Margaret, MD
Mernick, Mitchel, MD
Udesky, Robert A., MD
Vizel-Schwartz, Monique, MD

Nephrology

Nicolaides, Maria N:, MD
Rodman, John S., MD

OB/GYN

Adler, Alan A., MD
Bello, Gaetano, MD
Berman, Alvin, MD
Brodman, Michael, MD
Carlon, Anne, MD
Cavalli, Adele, MD
Chin Quee, Karlene, MD
Corio, Laura, MD
Creatura, Chris, MD
Faroqui, Raufa, MD
Fischer, Ilene M., MD
Friedman, Lynn, MD
Goldman, Gary H., MD
Gruss, Leslie, MD
Ho, Alison, MD
Hobgood, Laura S., MD
Lebowitz, Nancy, MD
Livoti, Carol, MD
Manos, Ellen, MD
Nachamie, Rebecca, MD
Park, Brian, MD
Reiss, Ronald J., MD
Sassoon, Albert K., MD, MPH
Selick, Caryn E., MD
Sillay, Laila R., MD
Wenger, Judith, MD
Yale, Suzanne, MD
Zilberstein, Inga, MD

Pediatric Allergy

Lazarus, Herbert, MD

Pediatric Endocrinology

Rosenbaum, Michael, MD
Softness, Barney, MD

Pediatric Pulmonology

Elbirt-Bender, Paula, MD

Pediatric Rheumatology

Lazarus, Herbert, MD

Pediatrics

Coffey, Robert J., MD
Daar, Eileen R., MD
Elbirt-Bender, Paula, MD
Goldstein, Judith, MD
Grunfeld, Paul, MD
Kahn, Max A., MD
Kessler, Ruth E., MD
Khanna, Kussum, MD
Lantz, Howard, MD
Lazarus, Herbert, MD
Murphy, Ramon J. C., MD
Pasquariello, Palmo, MD
Pegler, Cynthia, MD
Popper, Laura, MD
Rosenbaum, Michael, MD
Rosenfeld, Suzanne, MD
Schwartz, Stephen, MD
Seed, Wm., MD
Skog, Donald R., MD
Smith, David I., MD
Snyder, Fredrick E., MD
Softness, Barney, MD
Spielman, Gerald, MD
Stein, Barry B., MD
Sussman, Elihu, MD

Van Gilder, Max, MD
Weller, Alan S., MD
Wishnick, Marcia M., MD

Physical Medicine & Rehabilitation

Solomon, David Y., MD

Pulmonology

Abrams, Robert S., MD
Adler, Jack J., MD
Bregman, Zachary, MD
Falk, George A., MD
Hammer, David, MD
Horovitz, H. Leonard, MD
Keller, Raymond S., MD
Konecky, Alan, MD
Nash, Thomas W., MD
Posner, David H., MD
Schwartz, Lawrence P., MD
Woronoff, Richard S., MD

Rheumatolgy

Bernstein, Donald H., MD
Bernstein, Stephen J., MD
Kramer, Sara, MD
Leventhal, Gerald H., MD
Radin, Allen, MD

Doctor Information
and Scores

Abrams, Robert S., M.D.

INTERNAL MEDICINE · PULMONOLOGY

DOCTOR	OFFICE	OVERALL
8.3	**8.0**	**8.2**

LANGUAGES	MEDICAL SCHOOL	HOSPITAL AFFILIATIONS
Dutch	NY Med. '83	Lenox Hill
French		Mt. Sinai
Spanish		

Posner, Abrams & Bos MD PC
178 East 85 St
861-8976

GENERAL OFFICE INFORMATION	HMO/PPO
First Visit: _____ $250	Blue Choice
Regular Visit: ___ $75	Chubb
Accessible: _____ Yes	Oxford
Interpreters· ___ No	PHS/Guardian
Medicare: _____ Yes	
Medicaid: _____ No	
Evenings: _____ No	
Saturdays: _____ No	
AmEx: _____ Yes	
Visa/MC: _____ Yes	

PATIENT COMMENTS

He's a young, vibrant MD that
I recommend to my colleagues
and
he's helpful and takes your
problems very seriously.

Adler, Alan A., M.D.

OB/GYN

DOCTOR	OFFICE	OVERALL
8.3	**8.3**	**8.5**

LANGUAGES	MEDICAL SCHOOL	HOSPITAL AFFILIATIONS
Spanish	NYU '89	Mt. Sinai

Alan A. Adler, MD
70 East 90 St.
426-5366

GENERAL OFFICE INFORMATION	HMO/PPO
First Visit: _____ $180	Aetna/USH
Regular Visit: __ $120	Cigna
Accessible: _____ Yes	Magna Care
Interpreters: ____ No	Multiplan
Medicare: _____ No	Oxford
Medicaid: _____ No	PHS/Guardian
Evenings: _____ Yes	Premier Preferred
Saturdays: _____ No	PHCS
AmEx: _____ Yes	United Healthcare
Visa/MC: _____ Yes	

PATIENT COMMENTS

He takes as much time as
needed, is never in a hurry
and is great, and I really
enjoy him.

Adler, Howard, M.D.

GASTROENTEROLOGY · INTERNAL MEDICINE

DOCTOR	OFFICE	OVERALL
9.0	**8.6**	**9.0**

LANGUAGES	MEDICAL SCHOOL	HOSPITAL AFFILIATIONS
	Einstein '60	Beth Israel North

Howard Adler, MD
35 Sutton Pl.
421-3696

GENERAL OFFICE INFORMATION	HMO/PPO
First Visit: _____ $250	Blue Choice
Regular Visit: __ $100	Oxford
Accessible: _____ No	
Interpreters: ____ No	
Medicare: _____ No	
Medicaid: _____ No	
Evenings: _____ No	
Saturdays: _____ No	
AmEx: _____ No	
Visa/MC: _____ No	

PATIENT COMMENTS

Most say that:
he's the best of the best
I like him because he is into
sports and keeps active so he
can relate to his patients.
But some say:
the office staff is rude.

Adler, Jack J., M.D.

DOCTOR	OFFICE	OVERALL
7.5	7.1	7.8

INTERNAL MEDICINE · PULMONOLOGY

LANGUAGES	MEDICAL SCHOOL	HOSPITAL AFFILIATIONS
	Chicago '58	Beth Israel North
		Mount Sinai

AHB Pulmonary Associates
19 East 80 St
535-3622

GENERAL OFFICE INFORMATION		HMO/PPO
First Visit:	$325	Blue Choice
Regular Visit:	$120	Oxford
Accessible:	Yes	PHS/Guardian
Interpreters:	No	PHCS
Medicare:	Yes	Pru Care
Medicaid:	No	Sanus
Evenings:	Yes	
Saturdays:	No	
AmEx:	No	
Visa/MC:	No	

PATIENT COMMENTS

Not bad.
I would recommend him.

Adler, Mitchell A., M.D.

DOCTOR	OFFICE	OVERALL
8.1	8.5	8.7

INTERNAL MEDICINE

LANGUAGES	MEDICAL SCHOOL	HOSPITAL AFFILIATIONS
	NYU '80	NYU

Murray Hill Medical Group
317 East 34 St
726-7499

GENERAL OFFICE INFORMATION		HMO/PPO
First Visit:	n/a	Chubb
Regular Visit:	n/a	Oxford
Accessible:	Yes	
Interpreters:	No	
Medicare:	Yes	
Medicaid:	No	
Evenings:	No	
Saturdays:	No	
AmEx:	Yes	
Visa/MC:	Yes	

PATIENT COMMENTS

Gentle and tries to help me as well as he can.

Aguero, Jose, M.D.

DOCTOR	OFFICE	OVERALL
8.5	8.4	9.0

FAMILY PRACTICE

LANGUAGES	MEDICAL SCHOOL	HOSPITAL AFFILIATIONS
Italian	Spain 76	Beth Israel
Russian		St Luke's-Roosevelt
Spanish		

Jose Aguero, MD
50 West 77 St.
579-6000

PATIENT COMMENTS

GENERAL OFFICE INFORMATION		HMO/PPO
First Visit:	$150	Aetna/USH
Regular Visit:	$75	Chubb
Accessible:	Yes	Cigna
Interpreters:	No	Empire
Medicare:	Yes	Magna Care
Medicaid:	No	Oxford
Evenings:	Yes	PHS/Guardian
Saturdays:	Yes	PHCS
AmEx:	No	
Visa/MC:	Yes	

Excellent, broad knowledge of clinical medicine and medications and very personable with a great sense of humor.

Great bedside manner but always overbooked.

Altman, Kenneth A., M.D.

GASTROENTEROLOGY · INTERNAL MEDICINE

DOCTOR	OFFICE	OVERALL
9.1	8.9	9.6

LANGUAGES	MEDICAL SCHOOL	HOSPITAL AFFILIATIONS
French	Columbia '54	St Luke's-Roosevelt
German		
Hebrew		
Spanish		
Yiddish		

Kenneth A. Altman, MD
425 West 59 St
246-1264

GENERAL OFFICE INFORMATION		HMO/PPO
First Visit:	n/a	Private Practice
Regular Visit:	n/a	
Accessible:	Yes	
Interpreters:	No	
Medicare:	No	
Medicaid:	No	
Evenings:	No	
Saturdays:	No	
AmEx:	No	
Visa/MC:	No	

PATIENT COMMENTS

Very good with a good personality, all my friends go there.

Ament, Joseph D., M.D.

INTERNAL MEDICINE

DOCTOR	OFFICE	OVERALL
7.0	7.3	6.5

LANGUAGES	MEDICAL SCHOOL	HOSPITAL AFFILIATIONS
Spanish	Syracuse '79	Beth Israel North

Joseph Ament, MD
1045 Park Ave
410-6200

GENERAL OFFICE INFORMATION		HMO/PPO
First Visit:	n/a	Aetna/USH
Regular Visit:	n/a	Blue Choice
Accessible:	Yes	Local 1199
Interpreters:	No	Local 32BJ
Medicare:	Yes	Unified
Medicaid:	No	
Evenings:	Yes	
Saturdays:	No	
AmEx:	No	
Visa/MC:	No	

PATIENT COMMENTS

You have to wait a long time, he has a lot of patients.

Amiraian, Richard H., M.D.

INTERNAL MEDICINE

DOCTOR	OFFICE	OVERALL
7.4	7.2	7.3

LANGUAGES	MEDICAL SCHOOL	HOSPITAL AFFILIATIONS
	SUNY, Buffalo '83	St Luke's-Roosevelt
		St. Vincent's

West Park Medical Group
1886 Broadway
247-8100

GENERAL OFFICE INFORMATION		HMO/PPO
First Visit:	$200	Aetna/USH
Regular Visit:	$150	Blue Choice
Accessible:	Yes	Health Ease
Interpreters:	No	HealthNet
Medicare:	Yes	Oxford
Medicaid:	No	
Evenings:	Yes	
Saturdays:	Yes	
AmEx:	Yes	
Visa/MC:	Yes	

PATIENT COMMENTS

Some say:

he provides service as expected and is nice and attentive, but the office staff is terrible.

Another says:

his office is like a factory, no concern for his patients.

Andersen Holly, S., M.D.

CARDIOLOGY · INTERNAL MEDICINE

DOCTOR	OFFICE	OVERALL
9.3	8.3	9.4

LANGUAGES	MEDICAL SCHOOL	HOSPITAL AFFILIATIONS
French	Rochester '89	NY Hospital-Cornell
German		
Romanian		
Spanish		

Cornell Cardiology
Consultants
125 East 72 St.
628-6100

GENERAL OFFICE INFORMATION | **HMO/PPO**

First Visit: _____ n/a   Oxford
Regular Visit: ___ n/a
Accessible: _____ No
Interpreters: ____ No
Medicare: _____ Yes
Medicaid: _____ No
Evenings: _____ No
Saturdays: _____ No
AmEx: _____ Yes
Visa/MC: _____ Yes

PATIENT COMMENTS

Mucho, mucho satisfied.

Arons, Elliot, M.D.

GASTROENTEROLOGY · INTERNAL MEDICINE

DOCTOR	OFFICE	OVERALL
7.5	8.0	7.6

LANGUAGES	MEDICAL SCHOOL	HOSPITAL AFFILIATIONS
Spanish	NY Med. '78	St Luke's-Roosevelt

Blye & Elliot Arens, MDs
123 West 86 St
877-2833

GENERAL OFFICE INFORMATION | **HMO/PPO**

First Visit: _____ $100   Aetna/USH
Regular Visit: ___ $85   Blue Choice
Accessible: _____ Yes   Chubb
Interpreters: ____ No   Cigna
Medicare: _____ Yes   Oxford
Medicaid: _____ No
Evenings: _____ Yes
Saturdays: _____ No
AmEx: _____ Yes
Visa/MC: _____ Yes

PATIENT COMMENTS

He's straightforward, no BS.

Very practically-oriented rather than technically-oriented

His nurse/practitioner is excellent and very attentive.

Attia, Albert, M.D.

GASTROENTEROLOGY · INTERNAL MEDICINE

DOCTOR	OFFICE	OVERALL
7.2	7.5	7.7

LANGUAGES	MEDICAL SCHOOL	HOSPITAL AFFILIATIONS
Spanish	Cornell '58	St Luke's-Roosevelt

Albert Attia MD PC
350 West 58 St
307-7210

GENERAL OFFICE INFORMATION | **HMO/PPO**

First Visit: _____ $300   Cambridge
Regular Visit: __ $100   Chubb
Accessible: _____ Yes   Cigna
Interpreters: ____ No   Empire
Medicare: _____ Yes   Magna Care
Medicaid: _____ No   Oxford
Evenings: _____ No   PHCS
Saturdays: _____ No   Pru Care
AmEx: _____ No
Visa/MC: _____ No

PATIENT COMMENTS

It's hard to get past his staff.

Babitz, Lisa E., M.D.

GERIATRICS · INTERNAL MEDICINE

	DOCTOR	OFFICE	OVERALL
	8.2	7.4	8.3

LANGUAGES	MEDICAL SCHOOL	HOSPITAL AFFILIATIONS
	Yale '81	St Luke's-Roosevelt

Lisa E. Babitz,, M.D.
457 West 57 St
265-1471

GENERAL OFFICE INFORMATION

		HMO/PPO
First Visit: _____ $150		Aetna/USH
Regular Visit: ___ $75		Blue Choice
Accessible: _____ No		Chubb
Interpreters: ____ No		Oxford
Medicare: _____ Yes		PHS/Guardian
Medicaid: _____ No		Pru Care
Evenings: _____ No		
Saturdays: _____ No		
AmEx: _____ No		
Visa/MC: _____ No		

PATIENT COMMENTS

Some say:

she really takes time with each patient. You never feel rushed.

But others say:

the doctor lacks interpersonal skills.

Bahr, Gerald S., M.D.

CRITICAL CARE · INTERNAL MEDICINE

	DOCTOR	OFFICE	OVERALL
	7.0	7.8	6.7

LANGUAGES	MEDICAL SCHOOL	HOSPITAL AFFILIATIONS
Italian	NY Med. '72	Beth Israel North
Spanish		Lenox Hill

Madison Medical Group
110 East 59 St.
583-2820

GENERAL OFFICE INFORMATION

		HMO/PPO
First Visit: _____ $135		Cigna
Regular Visit: __ $100		Oxford
Accessible: _____ Yes		United Healthcare
Interpreters: ____ No		
Medicare: _____ Yes		
Medicaid: _____ No		
Evenings: _____ No		
Saturdays: _____ No		
AmEx: _____ Yes		
Visa/MC: _____ Yes		

PATIENT COMMENTS

Some say:

he's bland, not emotional and never goes the extra mile.

Others say:

phone calls are never returned and referrals take weeks.

Baiocco, Peter, M.D.

GASTROENTEROLOGY · INTERNAL MEDICINE

	DOCTOR	OFFICE	OVERALL
	9.0	8.1	9.6

LANGUAGES	MEDICAL SCHOOL	HOSPITAL AFFILIATIONS
French	Mt. Sinai, NY '78	Lenox Hill
Italian		
Spanish		

Peter J. Baiocco, M.D.
1317 Third Ave
734-8811

GENERAL OFFICE INFORMATION

		HMO/PPO
First Visit: _____ $175		Aetna/USH
Regular Visit: __ $100		Blue Choice
Accessible: _____ Yes		Cigna
Interpreters: ____ No		Healthsource
Medicare: _____ Yes		Magna Care
Medicaid: _____ No		Oxford
Evenings: _____ No		PHS/Guardian
Saturdays: _____ No		PHCS
AmEx: _____ Yes		
Visa/MC: _____ No		

PATIENT COMMENTS

Some say:

he's very attentive and dedicated.

Another says:

he's considerate of money. If one prescription costs more than an equivalent one, he'll give you the cheaper one.

Bardes, Charles L., M.D.

DOCTOR	OFFICE	OVERALL
7.4	**7.2**	**7.4**

INTERNAL MEDICINE

LANGUAGES	MEDICAL SCHOOL	HOSPITAL AFFILIATIONS
	U of PA '86	NY Hospital-Cornell

Charles L. Bardes, MD
525 East 68 St
746-1333

GENERAL OFFICE INFORMATION

		HMO/PPO
First Visit: _____ $250		Aetna/USH
Regular Visit: ___ $90		Blue Choice
Accessible: _____ Yes		NYC Care
Interpreters: ____ No		Oxford
Medicare: _____ Yes		PHCS
Medicaid: _____ No		Unified
Evenings: _____ No		
Saturdays: _____ No		
AmEx: _____ No		
Visa/MC: _____ Yes		

PATIENT COMMENTS

Regular checkups have to be scheduled 3 months ahead, which I think is too long.

He takes on too many appointments and spends no more than 10 minutes for a female check-up.

Barnes, Edward, M.D.

DOCTOR	OFFICE	OVERALL
8.3	**7.6**	**8.0**

INTERNAL MEDICINE

LANGUAGES	MEDICAL SCHOOL	HOSPITAL AFFILIATIONS
Spanish	Mt. Sinai, NY '84	Joint Diseases
		NYU

Murray Hill Medical Group
317 East 34 St
726-7434

GENERAL OFFICE INFORMATION

		HMO/PPO
First Visit: _____ $260		Aetna/USH
Regular Visit: ___ n/a		Healthsource
Accessible: _____ Yes		Oxford
Interpreters: ____ No		United Healthcare
Medicare: _____ Yes		
Medicaid: _____ No		
Evenings: _____ Yes		
Saturdays: _____ No		
AmEx: _____ Yes		
Visa/MC: _____ Yes		

PATIENT COMMENTS

Most say:

he's very personable and a good guy with a very caring, pleasant office.

Baskin, David H., M.D.

DOCTOR	OFFICE	OVERALL
8.4	**7.8**	**8.4**

INTERNAL MEDICINE

LANGUAGES	MEDICAL SCHOOL	HOSPITAL AFFILIATIONS
Spanish	Boston U. '82	Columbia Presbyterian
		St Luke's-Roosevelt

Manhattan West Medical, PC
185 West End Ave
595-7701

GENERAL OFFICE INFORMATION

		HMO/PPO
First Visit: _____ $300		Aetna/USH
Regular Visit: __ $125		Healthsource
Accessible: _____ Yes		Oxford
Interpreters: ____ No		PHS/Guardian
Medicare: _____ Yes		Pru Care
Medicaid: _____ No		United Healthcare
Evenings: _____ Yes		
Saturdays: _____ No		
AmEx: _____ No		
Visa/MC: _____ No		

PATIENT COMMENTS

He's very attentive and nice.

Within 2 hours calls are returned.

Bauchman, Gail, M.D.

DOCTOR	OFFICE	OVERALL
7.9	8.0	8.7

FAMILY PRACTICE

LANGUAGES	MEDICAL SCHOOL	HOSPITAL AFFILIATIONS
	SUNY, Stony Brook '85	Mount Sinai St Luke's-Roosevelt

Gail Bauchman, MD
50 West 77 St.
579-0955

GENERAL OFFICE INFORMATION	HMO/PPO
First Visit: _____ n/a	
Regular Visit: ___ n/a	
Accessible: _____ n/a	
Interpreters: ____ n/a	
Medicare: _____ n/a	
Medicaid: _____ n/a	
Evenings: _____ n/a	
Saturdays: _____ n/a	
AmEx: _____ n/a	
Visa/MC: _____ n/a	

PATIENT COMMENTS

Overall excellent but her fees should have been explained in advance.

Bearnot, Robert, M.D.

DOCTOR	OFFICE	OVERALL
8.1	6.2	7.8

GASTROENTEROLOGY · INTERNAL MEDICINE

LANGUAGES	MEDICAL SCHOOL	HOSPITAL AFFILIATIONS
Spanish	NYU '75	NYU Downtown

Robert Bearnot, MD
245 East 35 St
684-3601

GENERAL OFFICE INFORMATION	HMO/PPO
First Visit: _____ $175	
Regular Visit: ___ n/a	
Accessible: _____ Yes	
Interpreters: ____ No	
Medicare: _____ Yes	
Medicaid: _____ No	
Evenings: _____ Yes	
Saturdays: _____ No	
AmEx: _____ No	
Visa/MC: _____ No	

PATIENT COMMENTS

A hard working, conscientious doctor.

Beautyman, Elizabeth J., M.D.

DOCTOR	OFFICE	OVERALL
8.1	8.1	8.8

HEMATOLOGY · INTERNAL MEDICINE

LANGUAGES	MEDICAL SCHOOL	HOSPITAL AFFILIATIONS
	Albany Medical College '78	St Luke's-Roosevelt

Elizabeth J. Beautyman, MD
16 East 90 St
722-4634

GENERAL OFFICE INFORMATION	HMO/PPO
First Visit: _____ n/a	Chubb
Regular Visit: ___ n/a	Multiplan
Accessible: ____ No	Oxford
Interpreters: ____ No	
Medicare: _____ Yes	
Medicaid: _____ No	
Evenings: _____ No	
Saturdays: _____ No	
AmEx: _____ Yes	
Visa/MC: _____ No	

PATIENT COMMENTS

She's good although not super-friendly but very competent.

I have confidence in her.

Beitler, Martin, M.D.

	DOCTOR	OFFICE	OVERALL
INTERNAL MEDICINE	**8.3**	**8.3**	**8.3**

LANGUAGES	MEDICAL SCHOOL	HOSPITAL AFFILIATIONS
	Mt. Sinai, NY '85	Beth Israel

Martin Beitler, MD
115 Spring St
431-8990

GENERAL OFFICE INFORMATION

		HMO/PPO
First Visit: ____ $125		Oxford
Regular Visit: __ $110		
Accessible: ____ Yes		
Interpreters: ____ Yes		
Medicare: _____ No		
Medicaid: _____ No		
Evenings: _____ No		
Saturdays: _____ Yes		
AmEx: _____ No		
Visa/MC: _____ Yes		

PATIENT COMMENTS

All business, no chit-chat.

Thoroughly professional and smart, willing to listen but conservative in his views.

You can get appointments right away.

Beitner, Orit, M.D.

	DOCTOR	OFFICE	OVERALL
GYNECOLOGY	**7.4**	**9.2**	**8.0**

LANGUAGES	MEDICAL SCHOOL	HOSPITAL AFFILIATIONS
French	Sackler, Tel Aviv '88	St Luke's-Roosevelt
Hebrew		
Russian		
Spanish		

Museum Medical Institute
211 Central Park West
877-3120

GENERAL OFFICE INFORMATION

		HMO/PPO
First Visit: ____ $125		Private Practice
Regular Visit: __ $100		
Accessible: ____ No		
Interpreters: ____ No		
Medicare: _____ No		
Medicaid: _____ No		
Evenings: _____ Yes		
Saturdays: _____ Yes		
AmEx: _____ Yes		
Visa/MC: _____ Yes		

PATIENT COMMENTS

Some say:
she's wonderful and gentle, always pleasant and makes you feel taken care of.

Others say:
I would have rather met her before I was asked to put on the "gown" and she skimmed over details

Belenkov, Elliot, M.D.

	DOCTOR	OFFICE	OVERALL
INTERNAL MEDICINE · MEDICAL ONCOLOGY	**8.4**	**8.5**	**8.7**

LANGUAGES	MEDICAL SCHOOL	HOSPITAL AFFILIATIONS
Russian	Baku, Russia '76	Beth Israel North
Spanish		Lenox Hill
		NY Hospital-Cornell

Elliot M. Belenkov, MD
178 East 85 St.
472-5500

GENERAL OFFICE INFORMATION

		HMO/PPO
First Visit: ____ $150		Blue Choice
Regular Visit: __ $100		Cigna
Accessible: ____ Yes		Health Ease
Interpreters: ____ No		HealthNet
Medicare: _____ Yes		Magna Care
Medicaid: _____ No		Oxford
Evenings: _____ Yes		Pru Care
Saturdays: _____ No		United Healthcare
AmEx: _____ Yes		
Visa/MC: _____ No		

PATIENT COMMENTS

Most say:
he's professional and very concerned, tries to accommodate, very convenient.

But others say:
you need to follow-up on your own.

Bell, Evan T., M.D.

INFECTIOUS DISEASES · INTERNAL MEDICINE

DOCTOR	OFFICE	OVERALL
8.5	8.7	9.2

LANGUAGES	MEDICAL SCHOOL	HOSPITAL AFFILIATIONS
	Univ. of PA '80	Lenox Hill

Madison Medical Group
110 East 59 St.
583-2830

PATIENT COMMENTS

Go to him; he's excellent.

GENERAL OFFICE INFORMATION		HMO/PPO
First Visit:	n/a	
Regular Visit:	n/a	
Accessible:	n/a	
Interpreters:	n/a	
Medicare:	n/a	
Medicaid:	n/a	
Evenings:	n/a	
Saturdays:	n/a	
AmEx:	n/a	
Visa/MC:	n/a	

Bello, Gaetano, M.D.

OB/GYN

DOCTOR	OFFICE	OVERALL
8.9	8.9	9.7

LANGUAGES	MEDICAL SCHOOL	HOSPITAL AFFILIATIONS
French	Mt. Sinai, NY '81	Mount Sinai
Italian		
Spanish		

Nachamie/Bello/Callipani
47 East 88 St
996-9800

PATIENT COMMENTS

I think the doctor is fantastic and has a terrific bedside manner.

Extremely enthusiastic and interested in his patients.

GENERAL OFFICE INFORMATION		HMO/PPO
First Visit:	$180	Private Practice
Regular Visit:	$110	
Accessible:	Yes	
Interpreters:	Yes	
Medicare:	Yes	
Medicaid:	No	
Evenings:	Yes	
Saturdays:	Yes	
AmEx:	No	
Visa/MC:	Yes	

Bendo, Dominick, M.D.

INTERNAL MEDICINE

DOCTOR	OFFICE	OVERALL
8.8	7.8	9.0

LANGUAGES	MEDICAL SCHOOL	HOSPITAL AFFILIATIONS
French	Padova, Italy '53	Downtown
Italian		St Luke's-Roosevelt
Spanish		

Dominick Bendo, MD
325 West End Ave
799-0966

PATIENT COMMENTS

Sees me after work and weekends.

Very busy man who goes out of his way for his patients.

Another says:

the staff can be rude.

GENERAL OFFICE INFORMATION		HMO/PPO
First Visit:	$80	Blue Choice
Regular Visit:	$60	Cigna
Accessible:	Yes	HealthNet
Interpreters:	No	Multiplan
Medicare:	Yes	Oxford
Medicaid:	No	
Evenings:	Yes	
Saturdays:	Yes	
AmEx:	No	
Visa/MC:	No	

Berman, Alvin, M.D.

DOCTOR	OFFICE	OVERALL
8.7	9.2	9.8

OB/GYN

LANGUAGES	MEDICAL SCHOOL	HOSPITAL AFFILIATIONS
Afrikkaans	Pretoria, S. Africa '70	Mount Sinai
Spanish		

Alvin Berman, MD PC
111 East 88 St
722-5757

GENERAL OFFICE INFORMATION		HMO/PPO
First Visit: _____ n/a		Oxford
Regular Visit: ___ n/a		Premier Preferred
Accessible: _____ Yes		PHCS
Interpreters: ____ No		Pru Care
Medicare: _____ Yes		
Medicaid: _____ No		
Evenings: _____ No		
Saturdays: _____ No		
AmEx: _____ No		
Visa/MC: _____ Yes		

PATIENT COMMENTS

He's caring, concerned and thorough.

Explains everything very well.

Berman, Joan K., M.D.

DOCTOR	OFFICE	OVERALL
8.7	8.7	9.3

GYNECOLOGY

LANGUAGES	MEDICAL SCHOOL	HOSPITAL AFFILIATIONS
Spanish	Arizona '78	Mount Sinai

Berman & Diamond, MDs
61 East 86 St
876-2200

GENERAL OFFICE INFORMATION		HMO/PPO
First Visit: _____ $185		Private Practice
Regular Visit: __ $135		
Accessible: _____ No		
Interpreters: ____ No		
Medicare: _____ No		
Medicaid: _____ No		
Evenings: _____ No		
Saturdays: _____ No		
AmEx: _____ No		
Visa/MC: _____ Yes		

PATIENT COMMENTS

She's very professional and personable. Fees are reasonable for a NY doc.

I trust her and think she is very sharp & perceptive. She knows her stuff!. Very nice, very friendly and generally interesting and interested.

Bernstein, Donald H., M.D.

DOCTOR	OFFICE	OVERALL
7.8	7.3	7.9

GERIATRICS · INTERNAL MEDICINE · RHEUMATOLOGY

LANGUAGES	MEDICAL SCHOOL	HOSPITAL AFFILIATIONS
Spanish	NY Med. '82	St. Vincent's

Donald H. Bernstein, MD
20 Fifth Ave
477-4510

GENERAL OFFICE INFORMATION		HMO/PPO
First Visit: _____ $200		Aetna/USH
Regular Visit: __ $125		Blue Choice
Accessible: _____ Yes		Oxford
Interpreters: ____ No		Pru Care
Medicare: _____ Yes		
Medicaid: _____ No		
Evenings: _____ No		
Saturdays: _____ No		
AmEx: _____ No		
Visa/MC: _____ No		

PATIENT COMMENTS

Some say:

he's nice and very experienced.

Others say:

he appears to be nice but should focus more on the patient.

Bernstein, Gerald, M.D.

ENDOCRINOLOGY · INTERNAL MEDICINE

DOCTOR	OFFICE	OVERALL
8.8	8.4	9.4

LANGUAGES	MEDICAL SCHOOL	HOSPITAL AFFILIATIONS
Cambodian	Tufts '59	Lenox Hill
Gaelic		
Spanish		

Mid Manhattan Medical Assoc.
35 East 75 St
288-1538

GENERAL OFFICE INFORMATION	HMO/PPO
First Visit: _____ $350	Oxford
Regular Visit: __ $110	
Accessible: ___ Yes	
Interpreters: ____ No	
Medicare: _____ Yes	
Medicaid: _____ No	
Evenings: _____ No	
Saturdays: _____ No	
AmEx: _____ No	
Visa/MC: _____ Yes	

PATIENT COMMENTS

Very friendly, makes you feel comfortable.

He has a lot of contacts in the industry—good for referrals.

Bernstein, Stephen J.

INTERNAL MEDICINE · RHEUMATOLOGY

DOCTOR	OFFICE	OVERALL
6.9	7.3	7.2

LANGUAGES	MEDICAL SCHOOL	HOSPITAL AFFILIATIONS
Italian	Rome, Italy '76	Beth Israel
Russian		Cabrini
Spanish		Joint Diseases
		Eye & Ear Infirmary

Pyramid Medical Assoc., PC
923 Fifth Ave
535-3222

GENERAL OFFICE INFORMATION	HMO/PPO
First Visit: _____ $200	Aetna/USH
Regular Visit: __ $125	Cigna
Accessible: _____ No	Healthsource
Interpreters: ____ No	Multiplan
Medicare: _____ No	Oxford
Medicaid: _____ No	Premier Preferred
Evenings: _____ Yes	PHCS
Saturdays: _____ No	United Healthcare
AmEx: _____ Yes	
Visa/MC: _____ Yes	

PATIENT COMMENTS

He tries hard, but he's so overworked.

A nice man, he really cares.

Smart, but a little self-centered.

Blye, Ellen, M.D.

INTERNAL MEDICINE

DOCTOR	OFFICE	OVERALL
6.4	6.7	6.3

LANGUAGES	MEDICAL SCHOOL	HOSPITAL AFFILIATIONS
Italian	NY Med '78	St Luke's-Roosevelt
Spanish		

Blye & Arons, MDs
123 West 86 St
877-2833

GENERAL OFFICE INFORMATION	HMO/PPO
First Visit: _____ n/a	Aetna/USH
Regular Visit: ___ n/a	Healthsource
Accessible: _____ Yes	Multiplan
Interpreters: ____ No	Oxford
Medicare: _____ Yes	
Medicaid: _____ No	
Evenings: _____ Yes	
Saturdays: _____ No	
AmEx: _____ Yes	
Visa/MC: _____ Yes	

PATIENT COMMENTS

Practices with an assembly line approach.

Too rushed, too business-like.

Brandon, Donald E., M.D.

`INTERNAL MEDICINE`

DOCTOR	OFFICE	OVERALL
8.8	7.8	8.7

LANGUAGES	MEDICAL SCHOOL	HOSPITAL AFFILIATIONS
Spanish	SW Texas '56	Beth Israel North NYU

Donald E Brandon, MD
115 East 61 St
838-4130

GENERAL OFFICE INFORMATION

First Visit: _____ n/a
Regular Visit: ___ n/a
Accessible: _____ Yes
Interpreters: ____ No
Medicare: _____ : No
Medicaid: _____ No
Evenings: _____ No
Saturdays: _____ No
AmEx: _____ No
Visa/MC: _____ No

HMO/PPO

Blue Choice
Cigna
Oxford
PHS/Guardian
United Healthcare

PATIENT COMMENTS

Braun, James F., D.O.

`FAMILY PRACTICE`

DOCTOR	OFFICE	OVERALL
8.5	8.6	8.9

LANGUAGES	MEDICAL SCHOOL	HOSPITAL AFFILIATIONS
Spanish	Health Sci Osteo, KC '79	St. Vincent's

Liberty Medical
314 West 14 St
243-1980

GENERAL OFFICE INFORMATION

First Visit: _____ $250
Regular Visit: ___ n/a
Accessible: _____ No
Interpreters: ____ No
Medicare: _____ Yes
Medicaid: _____ No
Evenings: _____ Yes
Saturdays: _____ No
AmEx: _____ Yes
Visa/MC: _____ Yes

HMO/PPO

Aetna/USH
Bank Street
Chubb
Oxford

PATIENT COMMENTS

I love my doctor and his staff is excellent.

A sweetheart, knows a lot.

But another says:

he doesn't spend enough time with patients.

Bregman, Zachary, M.D.

`INTERNAL MEDICINE · PULMONOLOGY`

DOCTOR	OFFICE	OVERALL
7.7	7.4	8.0

LANGUAGES	MEDICAL SCHOOL	HOSPITAL AFFILIATIONS
	U of PA '81	Beth Israel Cabrini

Zachary Bregman, MD
247 Third Ave, Suite 401
505-6663

GENERAL OFFICE INFORMATION

First Visit: _____ n/a
Regular Visit: ___ n/a
Accessible: _____ Yes
Interpreters: ____ No
Medicare: _____ Yes
Medicaid: _____ No
Evenings: _____ No
Saturdays: _____ No
AmEx: _____ No
Visa/MC: _____ Yes

HMO/PPO

Aetna/USH
Blue Choice
Cigna
Oxford
United Healthcare

PATIENT COMMENTS

Some patients say:

he's friendly, love his accent.

But others say:

his bedside manner is not right for me, I always have some anxiety and dissatisfaction in my visits.

Brettholz, Edward, M.D.

DOCTOR	OFFICE	OVERALL
6.1	**6.1**	**5.4**

GASTROENTEROLOGY · INTERNAL MEDICINE

LANGUAGES	MEDICAL SCHOOL	HOSPITAL AFFILIATIONS
Spanish	Geo. Wash. '79	Beth Israel

Gramercy Park Physicians
67 Irving Pl
353-2565

GENERAL OFFICE INFORMATION

First Visit: _____ $225
Regular Visit: __ $125
Accessible: _____ Yes
Interpreters: ____ No
Medicare: _____ Yes
Medicaid: _____ No
Evenings: _____ Yes
Saturdays: _____ Yes
AmEx: _____ Yes
Visa/MC: _____ Yes

HMO/PPO

Aetna/USH
Blue Choice
Oxford
PHS/Guardian
PHCS
Pru Care
Sanus
United Healthcare

PATIENT COMMENTS

Miscommunicated test results.
Doesn't listen to patients.

Brodman, Michael, M.D.

DOCTOR	OFFICE	OVERALL
8.3	**8.5**	**8.3**

OB/GYN

LANGUAGES	MEDICAL SCHOOL	HOSPITAL AFFILIATIONS
Spanish	Mt. Sinai, NY '82	Mount Sinai

Brodman, Friedman,
Beyers & Wain
Mt. Siniai Med. Center
5 East 98 St · 241-8762

GENERAL OFFICE INFORMATION

First Visit: _____ $180
Regular Visit: __ $110
Accessible: _____ Yes
Interpreters: ____ Yes
Medicare: _____ Yes
Medicaid: _____ No
Evenings: _____ Yes
Saturdays: _____ No
AmEx: _____ Yes
Visa/MC: _____ Yes

HMO/PPO

Aetna/USH
Oxford

PATIENT COMMENTS

He's great! Personable and
attentive.

Bruno, Peter J., M.D.

DOCTOR	OFFICE	OVERALL
8.3	**7.4**	**8.2**

INTERNAL MEDICINE

LANGUAGES	MEDICAL SCHOOL	HOSPITAL AFFILIATIONS
Italian	Hahnemann, PA '75	Beth Israel
Spanish		Lenox Hill

Madison Medical Group
110 East 59 St
583-2820

GENERAL OFFICE INFORMATION

First Visit: _____ n/a
Regular Visit: ___ n/a
Accessible: _____ Yes
Interpreters: ____ Yes
Medicare: _____ Yes
Medicaid: _____ Yes
Evenings: _____ No
Saturdays: _____ No
AmEx: _____ No
Visa/MC: _____ Yes

HMO/PPO

Aetna/USH
AHP
Blue Choice
Chubb
Oxford
POS
United Healthcare

PATIENT COMMENTS

A good doctor.
.

Buchel, Tamara L., M.D.

DOCTOR	OFFICE	OVERALL
8.8	8.6	8.8

FAMILY PRACTICE

LANGUAGES	MEDICAL SCHOOL	HOSPITAL AFFILIATIONS
Spanish	Manitoba, Canada '92	Beth Israel

Docs at NY Healthcare
55 East 34 St.
889-2119

GENERAL OFFICE INFORMATION	HMO/PPO
First Visit: _____ $100	Aetna/USH
Regular Visit: ___ $65	Cigna
Accessible: _____ Yes	Managed Healthcare
Interpreters: ____ No	Oxford
Medicare: _____ Yes	United Healthcare
Medicaid: _____ No	
Evenings: _____ No	
Saturdays: _____ No	
AmEx: _____ Yes	
Visa/MC: _____ Yes	

PATIENT COMMENTS

Personable and friendly.

Listens to you and doesn't prescribe drugs unnecessarily.

Buckner, Jeffrey A., M.D.

DOCTOR	OFFICE	OVERALL
6.6	7.4	6.7

HEMATOLOGY · INTERNAL MEDICINE · MEDICAL ONCOLOGY

LANGUAGES	MEDICAL SCHOOL	HOSPITAL AFFILIATIONS
Spanish	Mt. Sinai, NY '78	Beth Israel
Tagalog		NYU

Jeffrey Buckner, MD
35A East 35 St.
689-0040

GENERAL OFFICE INFORMATION	HMO/PPO
First Visit: _____ n/a	Blue Choice
Regular Visit: ___ n/a	Oxford
Accessible: _____ Yes	PHS/Guardian
Interpreters: ____ No	PHCS
Medicare: _____ Yes	Unified
Medicaid: _____ No	
Evenings: _____ No	
Saturdays: _____ No	
AmEx: _____ No	
Visa/MC: _____ No	

PATIENT COMMENTS

Impersonal, rushed, zero feedback and quite pompous, but knows his field.

Burns, Margaret M., M.D.

DOCTOR	OFFICE	OVERALL
8.9	8.6	9.0

INTERNAL MEDICINE

LANGUAGES	MEDICAL SCHOOL	HOSPITAL AFFILIATIONS
Spanish	Georgetown '77	St. Vincent's

Margaret M Burns MD
20 East 9 St
924-7873

GENERAL OFFICE INFORMATION	HMO/PPO
First Visit: _____ $95	Blue Choice
Regular Visit: ___ $85	Oxford
Accessible: _____ Yes	
Interpreters: ____ No	
Medicare: _____ No	
Medicaid: _____ No	
Evenings: _____ No	
Saturdays: _____ No	
AmEx: _____ No	
Visa/MC: _____ No	

PATIENT COMMENTS

Young, down to earth and very approachable.

Knows what's going on and very competent.

Cantor, Michael C., M.D.

GASTROENTEROLOGY · INTERNAL MEDICINE

DOCTOR	OFFICE	OVERALL
8.8	8.7	8.9

LANGUAGES	MEDICAL SCHOOL	HOSPITAL AFFILIATIONS
	Columbia '82	NY Hospital-Cornell

Michael C Cantor MD
310 East 72 St
472-3333

PATIENT COMMENTS

GENERAL OFFICE INFORMATION	HMO/PPO
First Visit: _____ $400	Private Practice
Regular Visit: __ $125	
Accessible: _____ Yes	
Interpreters: ____ Yes	
Medicare: _____ No	
Medicaid: _____ No	
Evenings: _____ No	
Saturdays: _____ No	
AmEx: _____ Yes	
Visa/MC: _____ Yes	

Has a warm, caring manner and answers questions patiently.

He is respectful, views patients as equals and has a great staff.

Carlon, Anne, M.D.

OB/GYN

DOCTOR	OFFICE	OVERALL
8.4	7.4	8.5

LANGUAGES	MEDICAL SCHOOL	HOSPITAL AFFILIATIONS
Spanish	Duke '83	NY Hospital-Cornell

Anne Carlon MD PC
235 East 67 St, Suite 204
988-8100

PATIENT COMMENTS

GENERAL OFFICE INFORMATION	HMO/PPO
First Visit: _____ $230	Private Practice
Regular Visit: __ $180	
Accessible: _____ Yes	
Interpreters: ____ No	
Medicare: _____ No	
Medicaid: _____ No	
Evenings: _____ No	
Saturdays: _____ No	
AmEx: _____ Yes	
Visa/MC: _____ Yes	

Very sweet and kind, very warm. Not all business.

She tries to do the best and to be the best.

Cavalli, Adele, M.D.

OB/GYN

DOCTOR	OFFICE	OVERALL
9.7	9.1	9.8

LANGUAGES	MEDICAL SCHOOL	HOSPITAL AFFILIATIONS
Spanish	Guadalajara, Mex '80	Lenox Hill
		St. Vincent's

Adele Cavalli MD
20 Fifth Ave, Suite 1D
353-0008

PATIENT COMMENTS

GENERAL OFFICE INFORMATION	HMO/PPO
First Visit: _____ $200	Private Practice
Regular Visit: __ $100	
Accessible: _____ No	
Interpreters: ____ Yes	
Medicare: _____ Yes	
Medicaid: _____ No	
Evenings: _____ No	
Saturdays: _____ Yes	
AmEx: _____ No	
Visa/MC: _____ No	

Never found a more personable doctor.

A 10!

Charap, Peter, M.D.

INTERNAL MEDICINE

DOCTOR	OFFICE	OVERALL
8.8	7.8	8.6

LANGUAGES	MEDICAL SCHOOL	HOSPITAL AFFILIATIONS
Spanish	Mt. Sinai, NY '84	Beth Israel
		Mount Sinai

Manhattan Primary Care
234 Central Park West
579-2200

GENERAL OFFICE INFORMATION		HMO/PPO
First Visit: _____ $225		Aetna/USH
Regular Visit: ___ $90		Chubb
Accessible: _____ Yes		Cigna
Interpreters: ____ No		Multiplan
Medicare: _____ Yes		NYC Care
Medicaid: _____ No		Oxford
Evenings: _____ Yes		PHS/Guardian
Saturdays: _____ No		Premier Preferred
AmEx: _____ Yes		PHCS
Visa/MC: _____ Yes		United Healthcare

PATIENT COMMENTS

Friendly, personable, didn't feel rushed.

Chin Quee, Karlene, M.D.

OB/GYN

DOCTOR	OFFICE	OVERALL
8.4	8.7	8.7

LANGUAGES	MEDICAL SCHOOL	HOSPITAL AFFILIATIONS
Spanish	SUNY, Stony Brook '82	Lenox Hill

Karlene Chin Quee, MD
880 Fifth Ave
861-3130

GENERAL OFFICE INFORMATION		HMO/PPO
First Visit: _____ $350		Private Practice
Regular Visit: __ $210		
Accessible: _____ No		
Interpreters: ____ Yes		
Medicare: _____ No		
Medicaid: _____ No		
Evenings: _____ Yes		
Saturdays: _____ No		
AmEx: _____ Yes		
Visa/MC: _____ Yes		

PATIENT COMMENTS

She is nice and makes me feel comfortable and tries to be sweet in a hurried fashion.

A double "10" on being personal.

Cho, Sam K., M.D.

GENERAL SURGERY

DOCTOR	OFFICE	OVERALL
8.6	8.5	8.6

LANGUAGES	MEDICAL SCHOOL	HOSPITAL AFFILIATIONS
Japanese	Yonsei Sev., Korea '54	Beth Israel North
Korean		

Sam K Cho, MD
449 East 58 St
751-1284

GENERAL OFFICE INFORMATION		HMO/PPO
First Visit: _____ $125		Blue Choice
Regular Visit: ___ $75		Independent Health
Accessible: _____ Yes		Oxford
Interpreters: ____ No		
Medicare: _____ Yes		
Medicaid: _____ No		
Evenings: _____ No		
Saturdays: _____ No		
AmEx: _____ No		
Visa/MC: _____ No		

PATIENT COMMENTS

He addresses my problems without any "BS."

Very personable.

Chung, Bruce, M.D.

DOCTOR	OFFICE	OVERALL
8.9	8.1	8.7

FAMILY PRACTICE

LANGUAGES	MEDICAL SCHOOL	HOSPITAL AFFILIATIONS
Chinese	Wayne State '84	Beth Israel
Japanese		

City Care
160 East 32 St. #102
545-1888

GENERAL OFFICE INFORMATION	HMO/PPO
First Visit: ___ $125	Aetna/USH
Regular Visit: __ $100	Blue Choice
Accessible: _____ Yes	Cigna
Interpreters: ____ No	Magna Care
Medicare: _____ Yes	Multiplan
Medicaid: _____ Yes	Oxford
Evenings: _____ Yes	PHS/Guardian
Saturdays: _____ Yes	PHCS
AmEx: _____ Yes	Pru Care
Visa/MC: _____ Yes	

PATIENT COMMENTS

Excellent doctor. Very thorough, good listener, and attentive.

Very laid back, but effective.

Clements, Jerry, M.D.

DOCTOR	OFFICE	OVERALL
9.4	9.5	9.6

FAMILY PRACTICE

LANGUAGES	MEDICAL SCHOOL	HOSPITAL AFFILIATIONS
Spanish	Guadelajara, Mex. '83	Beth Israel
		St. Vincent's

Village Family Practice
25 Fifth Ave
477-1750

GENERAL OFFICE INFORMATION	HMO/PPO
First Visit: _____ $125	Private Practice
Regular Visit: ___ $85	
Accessible: _____ Yes	
Interpreters: ____ No	
Medicare: _____ No	
Medicaid: _____ No	
Evenings: _____ Yes	
Saturdays: _____ No	
AmEx: _____ Yes	
Visa/MC: _____ No	

PATIENT COMMENTS

Very courteous, makes you feel very comfortable.

Staff is good and I love my doctor.

Coffey, Robert J., M.D.

DOCTOR	OFFICE	OVERALL
8.1	8.3	8.4

PEDIATRICS

LANGUAGES	MEDICAL SCHOOL	HOSPITAL AFFILIATIONS
	Oklahoma '74	Beth Israel
		St. Vincent's

SOHO Pediatric Group
568 Broadway Suite 205
334-3366

GENERAL OFFICE INFORMATION	HMO/PPO
First Visit: _____ n/a	Aetna/USH
Regular Visit: ___ n/a	Blue Choice
Accessible: _____ Yes	Oxford
Interpreters: ____ No	PHS/Guardian
Medicare: _____ No	PHCS
Medicaid: _____ No	
Evenings: _____ Yes	
Saturdays: _____ Yes	
AmEx: _____ No	
Visa/MC: _____ Yes	

PATIENT COMMENTS

I like him very much and my son loves him, he's excellent

Cohen, Albert, M.D.

DOCTOR	OFFICE	OVERALL
5.5	**5.9**	**6.2**

INTERNAL MEDICINE

LANGUAGES	MEDICAL SCHOOL	HOSPITAL AFFILIATIONS
German	Lausanne, Switz. '59	St Luke's-Roosevelt
Italian		
Spanish		

Albert Cohen, MD
155 West 68 St
874-6767

GENERAL OFFICE INFORMATION

		HMO/PPO
First Visit: _____ $100		Blue Choice
Regular Visit: ___ $60		Chubb
Accessible: _____ Yes		Cigna
Interpreters: ____ No		MasterCare
Medicare: _____ Yes		Oxford
Medicaid: _____ No		PHS/Guardian
Evenings: _____ Yes		United Healthcare
Saturdays: _____ No		
AmEx: _____ No		
Visa/MC: _____ No		

PATIENT COMMENTS

I don't know why he's in the profession he's in.

Cohen, Robert L., M.D.

DOCTOR	OFFICE	OVERALL
8.1	**8.1**	**8.6**

INTERNAL MEDICINE

LANGUAGES	MEDICAL SCHOOL	HOSPITAL AFFILIATIONS
Spanish	Rush '75	St. Vincent's

Robert L Cohen, MD
314 West 14 St
620-0144

GENERAL OFFICE INFORMATION

		HMO/PPO
First Visit: _____ n/a		Blue Choice
Regular Visit: ___ n/a		Oxford
Accessible: _____ Yes		PHCS
Interpreters:.____ No		Pru Care
Medicare: _____ Yes		United Healthcare
Medicaid: _____ No		
Evenings: _____ No		
Saturdays: _____ No		
AmEx: _____ No		
Visa/MC: _____ No		

PATIENT COMMENTS

Most say:

he's extremely open, knowledgeable and easy to talk to and takes all questions and concerns very seriously.

Others say:

he's overbooked too much; short staffed.

Colt, Edward, M.D.

DOCTOR	OFFICE	OVERALL
6.4	**6.5**	**5.5**

ENDOCRINOLOGY · INTERNAL MEDICINE

LANGUAGES	MEDICAL SCHOOL	HOSPITAL AFFILIATIONS
Spanish	U London, UK '72	St Luke's-Roosevelt
		St. Vincent's

West Park Medical Group
1886 Broadway
247-8100

GENERAL OFFICE INFORMATION

		HMO/PPO
First Visit: _____ $200		Aetna/USH
Regular Visit: __ $175		Blue Choice
Accessible: _____ Yes		Health Ease
Interpreters: ____ No		Oxford
Medicare: _____ Yes		
Medicaid: _____ No		
Evenings: _____ Yes		
Saturdays: _____ Yes		
AmEx: _____ Yes		
Visa/MC: _____ Yes		

PATIENT COMMENTS

He's not too concerned; a bit too hasty.

Professional but lacking in bedside manner.

Corio, Laura, M.D.

DOCTOR	OFFICE	OVERALL
8.4	8.4	8.8

OB/GYN

LANGUAGES	MEDICAL SCHOOL	HOSPITAL AFFILIATIONS
Spanish	UMDNJ, Newark '78	Mount Sinai

Corio Morris Associates
60 East 88 St
860-6700

GENERAL OFFICE INFORMATION	HMO/PPO
First Visit: _____ $195	Chubb
Regular Visit: __ $150	Oxford
Accessible: _____ Yes	
Interpreters. _____ No	
Medicare: _____ Yes	
Medicaid: _____ No	
Evenings: _____ Yes	
Saturdays: _____ No	
AmEx: _____ Yes	
Visa/MC: _____ Yes	

PATIENT COMMENTS

She's excellent; I recommend her highly and have recommended her to friends who all say they feel the same way.

Creatura, Chris, M.D.

DOCTOR	OFFICE	OVERALL
8.7	8.8	9.1

OB/GYN

LANGUAGES	MEDICAL SCHOOL	HOSPITAL AFFILIATIONS
Italian	Harvard '86	NY Hospital-Cornell
Spanish		

Chris Creatura, MD PD
235 East 67 St.
722-2330

GENERAL OFFICE INFORMATION	HMO/PPO
First Visit: _____ $200	Private Practice
Regular Visit: __ $125	
Accessible: _____ Yes	
Interpreters: ____ No	
Medicare: _____ No	
Medicaid: _____ No	
Evenings: _____ No	
Saturdays: _____ No	
AmEx: _____ No	
Visa/MC: _____ No	

PATIENT COMMENTS

She's great, I highly recommend her. Very professional; tries to allay patient's concerns, very pleasant. Superb!

She delivered our child and was completely attentive . . . she stayed at the hospital for active labor.

Daar, Eileen R., M.D.

DOCTOR	OFFICE	OVERALL
9.3	9.0	9.2

PEDIATRICS

LANGUAGES	MEDICAL SCHOOL	HOSPITAL AFFILIATIONS
	Guadalajara, Mex. '79	Lenox Hill

Eileen R. Daar, MD
1009 Park Ave.
879-3473

GENERAL OFFICE INFORMATION	HMO/PPO
First Visit: _____ $95	Aetna/USH
Regular Visit: ___ $75	
Accessible: _____ Yes	
Interpreters: ____ No	
Medicare: _____ No	
Medicaid: _____ No	
Evenings: _____ Yes	
Saturdays: _____ No	
AmEx: _____ No	
Visa/MC: _____ No	

PATIENT COMMENTS

My children get along very well with her and she has a very pleasant office.

De Cotis, Sue Gene, M.D.

INTERNAL MEDICINE

DOCTOR	OFFICE	OVERALL
7.3	7.9	7.3

LANGUAGES	MEDICAL SCHOOL	HOSPITAL AFFILIATIONS
Spanish	NY Med '80	Beth Israel

Sue Gene De Cotis, MD
213 Madison Ave. #1B
685-3640

GENERAL OFFICE INFORMATION	HMO/PPO
First Visit: _____ n/a	
Regular Visit: ___ n/a	
Accessible: _____ Yes	
Interpreters: ____ No	
Medicare: _____ No	
Medicaid: _____ No	
Evenings: _____ Yes	
Saturdays: _____ No	
AmEx: _____ No	
Visa/MC: _____ No	

PATIENT COMMENTS

She's thorough and attentive and provides answers to all my questions.

Dellosso, John, M.D.

INTERNAL MEDICINE

DOCTOR	OFFICE	OVERALL
8.6	8.6	9.0

LANGUAGES	MEDICAL SCHOOL	HOSPITAL AFFILIATIONS
	NYU '91	

John Dellosso, MD
14 East 11 St.
645-8500

GENERAL OFFICE INFORMATION	HMO/PPO
First Visit: _____ n/a	
Regular Visit: ___ n/a	
Accessible: _____ n/a	
Interpreters: ____ n/a	
Medicare: _____ n/a	
Medicaid: _____ n/a	
Evenings: _____ n/a	
Saturdays: _____ n/a	
AmEx: _____ n/a	
Visa/MC: _____ n/a	

PATIENT COMMENTS

Young, very thorough and personable.

Demar, Leon K., M.D.

DERMATOLOGY

DOCTOR	OFFICE	OVERALL
7.8	8.5	7.8

LANGUAGES	MEDICAL SCHOOL	HOSPITAL AFFILIATIONS
Spanish	NYU '73	Beth Israel
		Columbia Presbyterian
		Lenox Hill
		St Luke's-Roosevelt

Leon K Demar, MD
985 Fifth Ave.
988-9010

GENERAL OFFICE INFORMATION	HMO/PPO
First Visit: _____ $125	Chubb
Regular Visit: ___ n/a	Multiplan
Accessible: _____ Yes	Oxford
Interpreters: ____ Yes	PHCS
Medicare: _____ Yes	United Healthcare
Medicaid: _____ No	
Evenings: _____ No	
Saturdays: _____ No	
AmEx: _____ No	
Visa/MC: _____ Yes	

PATIENT COMMENTS

Doctor is personable however I feel he is always in a rush.

When I ask questions, I feel he is giving a very quick answer so he can go on to his next patient.

Dhalla, Satish, M.D.

	DOCTOR	OFFICE	OVERALL
INTERNAL MEDICINE	8.4	8.6	8.3

LANGUAGES	MEDICAL SCHOOL	HOSPITAL AFFILIATIONS
	All India, Delhi '72	Downtown
		St. Vincent's

Satish Dhalla, MD
30 Fifth Ave
475-6223

GENERAL OFFICE INFORMATION	HMO/PPO
First Visit: _____ $130	Aetna/USH
Regular Visit: ___ $80	Cigna
Accessible: _____ Yes	United Healthcare
Interpreters: ____ No	
Medicare: _____ Yes	
Medicaid: _____ No	
Evenings: _____ No	
Saturdays: _____ No	
AmEx: _____ No	
Visa/MC: _____ No	

PATIENT COMMENTS

Serves coffee in waiting room.

Listens well and is efficient, but needs to tidy up office.

Diamond, Carol, M.D.

	DOCTOR	OFFICE	OVERALL
INTERNAL MEDICINE · MEDICAL ONCOLOGY	9.5	9.7	9.4

LANGUAGES	MEDICAL SCHOOL	HOSPITAL AFFILIATIONS
Spanish	Hahnemann, Pa '83	Mount Sinai

Carol Diamond, MD
285 West End Ave.
579-1200

GENERAL OFFICE INFORMATION	HMO/PPO
First Visit: _____ $200	Anthem Health
Regular Visit: __ $100	Blue Choice
Accessible: _____ Yes	Chubb
Interpreters: ____ No	Oxford
Medicare: _____ Yes	PHS/Guardian
Medicaid: _____ No	
Evenings: _____ Yes	
Saturdays: _____ No	
AmEx: _____ No	
Visa/MC: _____ No	

PATIENT COMMENTS

I recommend her highly, she knows a lot of experts who she can recommend.

Drapkin, Arnold, M.D.

	DOCTOR	OFFICE	OVERALL
INTERNAL MEDICINE	8.2	7.5	9.0

LANGUAGES	MEDICAL SCHOOL	HOSPITAL AFFILIATIONS
	SUNY, Syracuse '55	Mount Sinai

Arnold Drapkin, MD
1050 Fifth Ave.
289-0101

GENERAL OFFICE INFORMATION	HMO/PPO
First Visit: _____ n/a	
Regular Visit: ___ n/a	
Accessible: _____ n/a	
Interpreters: ____ n/a	
Medicare: _____ n/a	
Medicaid: _____ n/a	
Evenings: _____ n/a	
Saturdays: _____ n/a	
AmEx: _____ n/a	
Visa/MC: _____ n/a	

PATIENT COMMENTS

He's fantastic, he's great.

He's the best doctor I've ever seen.

Thorough, I have great confidence in his capability.

Dubin, Richard, M.D.

DOCTOR	OFFICE	OVERALL
7.1	7.0	7.7

GASTROENTEROLOGY · INTERNAL MEDICINE

LANGUAGES	MEDICAL SCHOOL	HOSPITAL AFFILIATIONS
Russian	Einstein '70	Beth Israel

Richard Dubin, MD
77 Park Ave
686-3720

PATIENT COMMENTS

GENERAL OFFICE INFORMATION	HMO/PPO
First Visit: _____ n/a	
Regular Visit: ___ n/a	
Accessible: _____ n/a	
Interpreters: ____ n/a	
Medicare: _____ n/a	
Medicaid: _____ n/a	
Evenings: _____ n/a	
Saturdays: _____ n/a	
AmEx: _____ n/a	
Visa/MC: _____ n/a	

Edwards, Colleen A., M.D.

DOCTOR	OFFICE	OVERALL
8.0	7.6	8.0

HEMATOLOGY · INTERNAL MEDICINE

LANGUAGES	MEDICAL SCHOOL	HOSPITAL AFFILIATIONS
Spanish	Univ. of PA '84	Beth Israel North
		Mount Sinai

Colleen A Edwards, MD
1050 Park Ave
410-9100

PATIENT COMMENTS

*Seems like she doesn't know
what she's talking about.*

I only go for referrals.

GENERAL OFFICE INFORMATION	HMO/PPO
First Visit: _____ $240	Aetna/USH
Regular Visit: ___ $90	Blue Choice
Accessible: _____ Yes	Cigna
Interpreters: ____ No	Health Ease
Medicare: _____ Yes	Oxford
Medicaid: _____ No	
Evenings: _____ No	
Saturdays: _____ No	
AmEx: _____ No	
Visa/MC: _____ No	

Elbirt-Bender, Paula, M.D.

DOCTOR	OFFICE	OVERALL
8.9	9.3	9.0

PEDIATRIC PULMONOLOGY · PEDIATRICS

LANGUAGES	MEDICAL SCHOOL	HOSPITAL AFFILIATIONS
Spanish	Hahnemann '79	Beth Israel
Yiddish		Lenox Hill
		Mount Sinai

MDS4KIDS
983 Park Ave
737-1155

PATIENT COMMENTS

*You never know how great
your doctor is until the time
of an emergency and she and
her partners have been
excellent.*

GENERAL OFFICE INFORMATION	HMO/PPO
First Visit: _____ $110	Private Practice
Regular Visit: ___ $95	
Accessible: _____ No	
Interpreters: ____ No	
Medicare: _____ No	
Medicaid: _____ No	
Evenings: _____ Yes	
Saturdays: _____ No	
AmEx: _____ Yes	
Visa/MC: _____ Yes	

Ellis, George C., M.D.

CARDIOLOGY · INTERNAL MEDICINE

	DOCTOR	OFFICE	OVERALL
	8.6	8.9	9.0

LANGUAGES	MEDICAL SCHOOL	HOSPITAL AFFILIATIONS
	Cornell '74	NY Hospital-Cornell

George C Ellis, MD
1185 Park Ave
722-6613

PATIENT COMMENTS

GENERAL OFFICE INFORMATION	HMO/PPO
First Visit: _____ $200	Private Practice
Regular Visit: ___ $90	
Accessible: _____ Yes	
Interpreters: ____ No	
Medicare: _____ No	
Medicaid: _____ No	
Evenings: _____ No	
Saturdays: _____ No	
AmEx: _____ No	
Visa/MC: _____ No	

Very competent; knows what he is doing. One of the best.

Falk, George A., M.D.

ALLERGY & IMMUNOLOGY · INTERNAL MEDICINE · PULMONOLOGY

	DOCTOR	OFFICE	OVERALL
	8.8	7.7	9.3

LANGUAGES	MEDICAL SCHOOL	HOSPITAL AFFILIATIONS
Russian	Harvard '64	NY Hospital-Cornell
Spanish		

George A. Falk, MD PC
232 East 66 St
371-2665

PATIENT COMMENTS

GENERAL OFFICE INFORMATION	HMO/PPO
First Visit: _____ n/a	Oxford
Regular Visit: ___ n/a	PHCS
Accessible: _____ No	
Interpreters: ____ No	
Medicare: _____ Yes	
Medicaid: _____ No	
Evenings: _____ No	
Saturdays: _____ No	
AmEx: _____ No	
Visa/MC: _____ No	

Attentive; genuinely cares about his patients.

Excellent follow-up. Will send you a note and call you on weekends.

Fallick, Nina, M.D.

INTERNAL MEDICINE

	DOCTOR	OFFICE	OVERALL
	7.2	7.5	6.5

LANGUAGES	MEDICAL SCHOOL	HOSPITAL AFFILIATIONS
	Cornell '86	Beth Israel North
		Mount Sinai

Nina Fallick, MD
70 East 90 St
476-0190

PATIENT COMMENTS

GENERAL OFFICE INFORMATION	HMO/PPO
First Visit: _____ $235	Aetna/USH
Regular Visit: __ $100	Blue Choice
Accessible: ___,___ Yes	Chubb
Interpreters: ____ No	Cigna
Medicare: _____ Yes	Oxford
Medicaid: _____ No	Premier Preferred
Evenings: _____ No	Unified
Saturdays: _____ No	
AmEx: _____ Yes	
Visa/MC: _____ Yes	

Very reluctant to provide referrals to specialists.

Did not explain the need for certain allergy medications and became vaguely hostile when I continued to question her.

Faroqui, Raufa, M.D.

DOCTOR	OFFICE	OVERALL
6.6	**6.2**	**7.2**

OB/GYN

LANGUAGES	MEDICAL SCHOOL	HOSPITAL AFFILIATIONS
	Karnatak, Egypt '64	Lenox Hill
		St Luke's-Roosevelt

Raufa Faroqui, MD
59 East 54 St
888-1870

GENERAL OFFICE INFORMATION

		HMO/PPO
First Visit: _____ n/a		
Regular Visit: ___ n/a		
Accessible: _____ n/a		
Interpreters: ____ n/a		
Medicare: _____ n/a		
Medicaid: _____ n/a		
Evenings: _____ n/a		
Saturdays: _____ n/a		
AmEx: _____ n/a		
Visa/MC: _____ n/a		

PATIENT COMMENTS

Overbooked, but competent and knowledgeable.

Fischer, Ilene M., M.D.

DOCTOR	OFFICE	OVERALL
8.3	**9.0**	**9.0**

OB/GYN

LANGUAGES	MEDICAL SCHOOL	HOSPITAL AFFILIATIONS
Spanish	Temple '87	Beth Israel

Murray Hill OB/GYN, LLP
150 East 32 St.
447-5330

GENERAL OFFICE INFORMATION

	HMO/PPO
First Visit: _____ $200	Aetna/USH
Regular Visit: __ $125	Blue Choice
Accessible: _____ Yes	Chubb
Interpreters: ____ No	Cigna
Medicare: _____ No	NYC Care
Medicaid: _____ No	Oxford
Evenings: _____ Yes	PHCS
Saturdays: _____ No	Pru Care
AmEx: _____ Yes	
Visa/MC: _____ Yes	

PATIENT COMMENTS

Strongly recommended.

Very personable, sane and communicative regarding health care and women's specific problems.

Fishbane-Mayer, Jill, M.D.

DOCTOR	OFFICE	OVERALL
9.1	**8.9**	**9.0**

GYNECOLOGY

LANGUAGES	MEDICAL SCHOOL	HOSPITAL AFFILIATIONS
	Mt. Sinai, NY '76	Mount Sinai

Jill Fishbane-Mayer, MD
4 East 95 St
348-1111

GENERAL OFFICE INFORMATION

	HMO/PPO
First Visit: _____ $185	Private Practice
Regular Visit: __ $140	
Accessible: _____ Yes	
Interpreters: ____ No	
Medicare: _____ Yes	
Medicaid: _____ No	
Evenings: _____ No	
Saturdays: _____ No	
AmEx: _____ No	
Visa/MC: _____ No	

PATIENT COMMENTS

Patients say:

she's professional, caring and attentive.

Takes her time with you and understands women's problems.

Fisher, Laura, M.D.

INFECTIOUS DISEASES · INTERNAL MEDICINE

DOCTOR	OFFICE	OVERALL
7.4	7.0	7.8

LANGUAGES	MEDICAL SCHOOL	HOSPITAL AFFILIATIONS
French	Brown '84	NY Hospital-Cornell
Hebrew		

Laura Fisher, MD
449 East 68 St
746-1771

GENERAL OFFICE INFORMATION	HMO/PPO
First Visit: _____ $300	Cigna
Regular Visit: __ $110	PHS/Guardian
Accessible: _____ Yes	PHCS
Interpreters: _ No	Unified
Medicare: _____ No	United Healthcare
Medicaid: _____ No	
Evenings: _____ No	
Saturdays: _____ No	
AmEx: _____ Yes	
Visa/MC: _____ Yes	

PATIENT COMMENTS

Great care dispatched with terrible service.

She did not help me when I was in an emergency situation.

Frankel, Etta B., M.D.

HEMATOLOGY · INTERNAL MEDICINE · MEDICAL ONCOLOGY

DOCTOR	OFFICE	OVERALL
6.4	7.3	6.2

LANGUAGES	MEDICAL SCHOOL	HOSPITAL AFFILIATIONS
Spanish	Columbia '79	St Luke's-Roosevelt

Etta B. Frankel, MD
425 West 59 St
523-7090

GENERAL OFFICE INFORMATION	HMO/PPO
First Visit: _____ $225	Aetna/USH
Regular Visit: __ $110	Blue Choice
Accessible: _____ Yes	Cigna
Interpreters: ____ No	Local 32BJ
Medicare: _____ Yes	Oxford
Medicaid: _____ No	Pru Care
Evenings: _____ No	United Healthcare
Saturdays: _____ No	
AmEx: _____ Yes	
Visa/MC: _____ Yes	

PATIENT COMMENTS

Very concerned, wants to make sure you are totally healthy.

An older person who tolerates no nonsense.

Franklin, Kenneth W., M.D.

CARDIOLOGY · INTERNAL MEDICINE

DOCTOR	OFFICE	OVERALL
8.9	8.5	9.6

LANGUAGES	MEDICAL SCHOOL	HOSPITAL AFFILIATIONS
French	Harvard '78	NY Hospital-Cornell
		Special Surgery

72 St. Medical Assoc. PC
310 East 72 St.
838-4854

GENERAL OFFICE INFORMATION	HMO/PPO
First Visit: _____ n/a	
Regular Visit: ___ n/a	
Accessible: _____ Yes	
Interpreters: ____ No	
Medicare: _____ No	
Medicaid: _____ No	
Evenings: _____ No	
Saturdays: _____ No	
AmEx: _____ No	
Visa/MC: _____ No	

PATIENT COMMENTS

A lucky find.

Fried, Richard P., M.D.

DOCTOR	OFFICE	OVERALL
8.6	8.3	9.3

INFECTIOUS DISEASES · INTERNAL MEDICINE

LANGUAGES	MEDICAL SCHOOL	HOSPITAL AFFILIATIONS
French	Columbia '68	St Luke's-Roosevelt

Mid-Manhattan Medical Assoc.
15 West 72 St
580-4840

PATIENT COMMENTS

GENERAL OFFICE INFORMATION	HMO/PPO
First Visit: _____ n/a	Aetna/USH
Regular Visit: ___ n/a	Chubb
Accessible: _____ Yes	Cigna
Interpreters: ____ No	Oxford
Medicare: _____ Yes	Pru Care
Medicaid: _____ No	United Healthcare
Evenings: _____ No	
Saturdays: _____ No	
AmEx: _____ No	
Visa/MC: _____ No	

Excellent doctor and very aware of different life styles and sensitive to what your particular needs would be.

I would recommend him.

A great doctor. Very thorough.

Friedman, Jeffrey P., M.D.

DOCTOR	OFFICE	OVERALL
9.0	8.3	9.1

INTERNAL MEDICINE

LANGUAGES	MEDICAL SCHOOL	HOSPITAL AFFILIATIONS
Spanish	NYU '83	Joint Diseases
		NYU

Murray Hill Medical Group, PC
317 East 34 St.
726-7440

PATIENT COMMENTS

GENERAL OFFICE INFORMATION	HMO/PPO
First Visit: _____ $250	Chubb
Regular Visit: ___ $80	Oxford
Accessible: _____ Yes	United Healthcare
Interpreters: ____ No	
Medicare: _____ Yes	
Medicaid: _____ No	
Evenings: _____ Yes	
Saturdays: _____ No	
AmEx: _____ Yes	
Visa/MC: _____ Yes	

Great doctor, incredibly organized and a family man.

Easy to get along with easy to tell your problems to.

Friedman, Lynn, M.D.

DOCTOR	OFFICE	OVERALL
8.5	8.5	9.0

OB/GYN

LANGUAGES	MEDICAL SCHOOL	HOSPITAL AFFILIATIONS
	NYU '84	Mount Sinai

Abramson, Brodman,
Friedman & Brasner
229 East 79 St
737-3282

PATIENT COMMENTS

GENERAL OFFICE INFORMATION	HMO/PPO
First Visit: _____ $175	Oxford
Regular Visit: __ $110	
Accessible: _____ Yes	
Interpreters: ____ Yes	
Medicare: _____ Yes	
Medicaid: _____ No	
Evenings: _____ Yes	
Saturdays: _____ No	
AmEx: _____ No	
Visa/MC: _____ Yes	

Furman, Alice, M.D.

INTERNAL MEDICINE

DOCTOR	OFFICE	OVERALL
8.1	7.8	7.7

LANGUAGES	MEDICAL SCHOOL	HOSPITAL AFFILIATIONS
Creole	Mt. Sinai, NY '90	Beth Israel
Spanish		Mount Sinai

Manhattan Primary Care
70 East 90 St.
426-0190

GENERAL OFFICE INFORMATION	HMO/PPO
First Visit: _____ $150	Aetna/USH
Regular Visit: __ $150	Oxford
Accessible: _____ Yes	United Healthcare
Interpreters: ____ No	
Medicare: _____ Yes	
Medicaid: _____ No	
Evenings: _____ Yes	
Saturdays: _____ No	
AmEx: _____ Yes	
Visa/MC: _____ Yes	

PATIENT COMMENTS

She's a young, courteous and intelligent doctor.

Gale, Robert K., M.D.

INFECTIOUS DISEASES · INTERNAL MEDICINE

DOCTOR	OFFICE	OVERALL
8.9	8.0	8.4

LANGUAGES	MEDICAL SCHOOL	HOSPITAL AFFILIATIONS
Spanish	NY Med '85	Downtown

Medical & Dental Assoc.
141 Fifth Ave
533-2400

GENERAL OFFICE INFORMATION	HMO/PPO
First Visit: _____ $150	Private Practice
Regular Visit: __ $125	
Accessible: _____ Yes	
Interpreters: ____ No	
Medicare: _____ Yes	
Medicaid: _____ No	
Evenings: _____ Yes	
Saturdays: _____ Yes	
AmEx: _____ Yes	
Visa/MC: _____ Yes	

PATIENT COMMENTS

Very friendly and generally concerned about your health.

Makes me feel really relaxed.

Geltman, Richard L., M.D.

HEMATOLOGY · INTERNAL MEDICINE · MEDICAL ONCOLOGY

DOCTOR	OFFICE	OVERALL
7.8	6.8	7.7

LANGUAGES	MEDICAL SCHOOL	HOSPITAL AFFILIATIONS
Spanish	Einstein '71	NY Hospital-Cornell

Richard L. Geltman, MD
55 East 86 St
860-3344

GENERAL OFFICE INFORMATION	HMO/PPO
First Visit: _____ $150	Blue Choice
Regular Visit: ___ $80	Oxford
Accessible: _____ Yes	PHS/Guardian
Interpreters: ____ No	
Medicare: _____ Yes	
Medicaid: _____ No	
Evenings: _____ No	
Saturdays: _____ No	
AmEx: _____ Yes	
Visa/MC: _____ Yes	

PATIENT COMMENTS

The doctor is great but the staff has to go.

Another says:

the staff must learn to be more courteous and sensitive.

Glick, Jeffrey, M.D.

INTERNAL MEDICINE

DOCTOR	OFFICE	OVERALL
7.3	7.6	7.6

LANGUAGES	MEDICAL SCHOOL	HOSPITAL AFFILIATIONS
Greek	G. Washington '88	Beth Israel
Italian		Lenox Hill
Spanish		Manhattan Eye & Ear

Pre-Operative Medical
Consultants
184 East 70 St
737-2270

PATIENT COMMENTS

Excellent doc for straights and gays. Good but expensive,

GENERAL OFFICE INFORMATION		HMO/PPO
First Visit:	n/a	Aetna/USH
Regular Visit:	n/a	Blue Choice
Accessible:	Yes	Cigna
Interpreters:	No	GHI
Medicare:	Yes	Healthsource
Medicaid:	Yes	Magna Care
Evenings:	No	National Health Plan
Saturdays:	No	Oxford
AmEx:	Yes	
Visa/MC:	Yes	

Goldberg, Edward S., M.D.

GASTROENTEROLOGY · INTERNAL MEDICINE

DOCTOR	OFFICE	OVERALL
9.1	8.6	9.0

LANGUAGES	MEDICAL SCHOOL	HOSPITAL AFFILIATIONS
Spanish	UMDNJ '87	Beth Israel North
		Lenox Hill

Edward S Goldberg, MD
121 East 60 St.
980-0800

PATIENT COMMENTS

He cares for the whole individual not just the one symptom or area of infection and nice, personable, explains things and speaks well.

Another says *service is great.*

I can call him at noon and get to see him at the end of the day.

GENERAL OFFICE INFORMATION		HMO/PPO
First Visit:	$200	Aetna/USH
Regular Visit:	$100	Blue Choice
Accessible:	Yes	Independent Health
Interpreters:	No	PHS/Guardian
Medicare:	Yes	
Medicaid:	No	
Evenings:	Yes	
Saturdays:	No	
AmEx:	Yes	
Visa/MC:	No	

Goldberg, Richard, M.D.

FAMILY PRACTICE

DOCTOR	OFFICE	OVERALL
7.7	7.5	7.9

LANGUAGES	MEDICAL SCHOOL	HOSPITAL AFFILIATIONS
Spanish	U Michigan '76	Beth Israel
		Cabrini

The Family Medical Group
of NY
77 West 15 St
206-7717

PATIENT COMMENTS

Usually on time for appointments. Extremely practical, very reassuring, efficient.

But others say:

he's usually rushed and needs to pay more attention to patients.

GENERAL OFFICE INFORMATION		HMO/PPO
First Visit:	$95	Aetna/USH
Regular Visit:	$55	Blue Choice
Accessible:	Yes	Cigna
Interpreters:	No	Oxford
Medicare:	Yes	Sanus
Medicaid:	No	Unified
Evenings:	No	United Healthcare
Saturdays:	No	
AmEx:	No	
Visa/MC:	No	

Golden, Flavia A., M.D.

INTERNAL MEDICINE

DOCTOR	OFFICE	OVERALL
9.2	8.8	9.6

LANGUAGES	MEDICAL SCHOOL	HOSPITAL AFFILIATIONS
Chinese French Spanish	NY Med '90	NY Hospital-Cornell

The Center for Women's
Health Care
1315 York Ave.
746-2062

GENERAL OFFICE INFORMATION	HMO/PPO
First Visit: _____ $250	Aetna/USH
Regular Visit: __ $150	Oxford
Accessible: _____ Yes	PHS/Guardian
Interpreters: ____ No	PHCS
Medicare: _____ Yes	
Medicaid: _____ No	
Evenings: _____ No	
Saturdays: _____ No	
AmEx: _____ Yes	
Visa/MC: _____ Yes	

PATIENT COMMENTS

Great doctor.

Personable, friendly, and feeling that she cares.

Goldman, Gary H., M.D.

OB/GYN

DOCTOR	OFFICE	OVERALL
8.5	9.4	9.2

LANGUAGES	MEDICAL SCHOOL	HOSPITAL AFFILIATIONS
Spanish	SUNY, Stony Brook '86	NY Hospital-Cornell

Gary H Goldman, MD
519 East 63 St, Suite 202
535-6100

GENERAL OFFICE INFORMATION	HMO/PPO
First Visit: _____ $315	Oxford
Regular Visit: __ $245	PHCS
Accessible: _____ Yes	
Interpreters: ____ No	
Medicare: _____ No	
Medicaid: _____ No	
Evenings: _____ No	
Saturdays: _____ No	
AmEx: _____ No	
Visa/MC: _____ Yes	

PATIENT COMMENTS

Makes you feel comfortable and is concerned about you and your problems.

Goldstein, Judith, M.D.

PEDIATRICS

DOCTOR	OFFICE	OVERALL
6.5	7.7	6.0

LANGUAGES	MEDICAL SCHOOL	HOSPITAL AFFILIATIONS
French German Italian	SUNY, Bklyn '72	Lenox Hill NY Hospital-Cornell

Judith Goldstein, MD PC
1111 Park Ave
369-4670

GENERAL OFFICE INFORMATION	HMO/PPO
First Visit: _____ $100	Blue Choice
Regular Visit: ___ $90	Chubb
Accessible: _____ No	Cigna
Interpreters: ____ No	Oxford
Medicare: _____ No	PHCS
Medicaid: _____ No	United Healthcare
Evenings: _____ Yes	
Saturdays: _____ Yes	
AmEx: _____ Yes	
Visa/MC: _____ Yes	

PATIENT COMMENTS

I dislike her, she is very unprofessional.

Another says:

I don't think the doctor gives the children enough time to know them personally.

Goodman, Karl, M.D.

GERIATRICS · INTERNAL MEDICINE

DOCTOR	OFFICE	OVERALL
8.3	7.7	7.6

LANGUAGES	MEDICAL SCHOOL	HOSPITAL AFFILIATIONS
Spanish	Guadalajara, Mex '81	Downtown
		St Luke's-Roosevelt

Central Park West
Medical Group
2 West 86 St
769-4149

PATIENT COMMENTS

Mostly prompt & excellent service. However, knowledge of a broad range of symptoms is lacking.

Constant referral to specialists.

GENERAL OFFICE INFORMATION	HMO/PPO
First Visit: _____ $98	Aetna/USH
Regular Visit: ___ $78	United Healthcare
Accessible: _____ Yes	
Interpreters: ___ No	
Medicare: _____ Yes	
Medicaid: _____ No	
Evenings: _____ No	
Saturdays: _____ Yes	
AmEx: _____ Yes	
Visa/MC: _____ Yes	

Graf, Jeffrey H., M.D.

CARDIOLOGY · INTERNAL MEDICINE

DOCTOR	OFFICE	OVERALL
8.8	8.8	8.8

LANGUAGES	MEDICAL SCHOOL	HOSPITAL AFFILIATIONS
German	NYU '80	Mount Sinai
Spanish		
Yiddish		

East Side Physicians, PC
1111 Park Ave
410-6001

PATIENT COMMENTS

Very helpful, great but his office is too small.

GENERAL OFFICE INFORMATION	HMO/PPO
First Visit: _____ $175	Aetna/USH
Regular Visit: ___ $90	Blue Choice
Accessible: _____ Yes	Chubb
Interpreters: ___ No	Cigna
Medicare: _____ Yes	HealthNet
Medicaid: _____ No	Oxford
Evenings: _____ No	PHS/Guardian
Saturdays: _____ No	United Healthcare
AmEx: _____ No	
Visa/MC: _____ Yes	

Grossman, Howard A., M.D.

INTERNAL MEDICINE

DOCTOR	OFFICE	OVERALL
8.4	9.3	8.4

LANGUAGES	MEDICAL SCHOOL	HOSPITAL AFFILIATIONS
	SUNY, Bklyn '83	St Luke's-Roosevelt

Howard A Grossman, MD
155 West 19 St.
929-2629

PATIENT COMMENTS

Excellent care; very knowledgeable about AIDS care.

Unfortunately a bit overworked.

GENERAL OFFICE INFORMATION	HMO/PPO
First Visit: _____ $300	Aetna/USH
Regular Visit: ___ $100	Cigna
Accessible: _____ Yes	Healthsource
Interpreters: ___ Yes	Oxford
Medicare: _____ Yes	PHS/Guardian
Medicaid: _____ No	
Evenings: _____ Yes	
Saturdays: _____ No	
AmEx: _____ Yes	
Visa/MC: _____ Yes	

Grunfeld, Paul, M.D.

PEDIATRICS

DOCTOR	OFFICE	OVERALL
8.3	**8.9**	**8.7**

LANGUAGES	MEDICAL SCHOOL	HOSPITAL AFFILIATIONS
German	Cluj, Romania '60	Lenox Hill
Hungarian		
Spanish		

Paul Grunfeld, MD, PC
1111 Park Ave
534-3000

GENERAL OFFICE INFORMATION	HMO/PPO
First Visit: _____ $120	Aetna/USH
Regular Visit: ___ $95	Blue Choice
Accessible: _____ Yes	Chubb
Interpreters: ____ No	Oxford
Medicare: _____ No	PHS/Guardian
Medicaid: _____ No	PHCS
Evenings: _____ Yes	Pru Care
Saturdays: _____ Yes	United Healthcare
AmEx: _____ Yes	
Visa/MC: _____ Yes	

PATIENT COMMENTS

Some say:

very nice but expensive doctor. Great with small kids.

Others say:

office is a little hectic at times; should space out appointments more.

Gruss, Leslie, M.D.

OB/GYN

DOCTOR	OFFICE	OVERALL
9.1	**8.9**	**9.6**

LANGUAGES	MEDICAL SCHOOL	HOSPITAL AFFILIATIONS
Hebrew	Med. Coll. of PA '83	Beth Israel
Spanish		

Downtown Women
OB/GYN Assoc,, LLP
568 Broadway
966-7600

GENERAL OFFICE INFORMATION	HMO/PPO
First Visit: _____ $200	Oxford
Regular Visit: __ $150	PHCS
Accessible: _____ Yes	Pru Care
Interpreters: ____ No	United Healthcare
Medicare: _____ Yes	
Medicaid: _____ No	
Evenings: _____ Yes	
Saturdays: _____ No	
AmEx: _____ No	
Visa/MC: _____ Yes	

PATIENT COMMENTS

Excellent doctor, whole practice is excellent. Very caring.

Called me in the hospital on her vacation to check on me.

Halper, Peter, M.D.

GERIATRICS · INTERNAL MEDICINE

DOCTOR	OFFICE	OVERALL
7.9	**8.0**	**8.0**

LANGUAGES	MEDICAL SCHOOL	HOSPITAL AFFILIATIONS
Spanish	U. Conn. '62	Beth Israel

Gramercy Park Physicians
67 Irving Pl
529-3424

GENERAL OFFICE INFORMATION	HMO/PPO
First Visit: _____ n/a	Aetna/USH
Regular Visit: ___ n/a	Oxford
Accessible: _____ Yes	
Interpreters: ____ No	
Medicare: _____ Yes	
Medicaid: _____ No	
Evenings: _____ Yes	
Saturdays: _____ Yes	
AmEx: _____ Yes	
Visa/MC: _____ Yes	

PATIENT COMMENTS

Some say:

Great interest, although expensive.

Others say:

he has a juvenile personality.

Hammer, David, M.D.

INTERNAL MEDICINE · PULMONOLOGY

	DOCTOR	OFFICE	OVERALL
	7.1	7.1	6.3

LANGUAGES	MEDICAL SCHOOL	HOSPITAL AFFILIATIONS
Spanish	Boston '71	Beth Israel

Gramercy Park Physicians
67 Irving Pl
353-3636

GENERAL OFFICE INFORMATION		HMO/PPO
First Visit:	n/a	Aetna/USH
Regular Visit:	n/a	Oxford
Accessible:	Yes	
Interpreters:	No	
Medicare:	Yes	
Medicaid:	No	
Evenings:	No	
Saturdays:	Yes	
AmEx:	Yes	
Visa/MC:	Yes	

PATIENT COMMENTS

He's fine but follows the HMO thing too closely.

Very rushed, very few words.

Harris, Lucinda A., M.D.

GASTROENTEROLOGY · INTERNAL MEDICINE

	DOCTOR	OFFICE	OVERALL
	7.9	7.8	8.0

LANGUAGES	MEDICAL SCHOOL	HOSPITAL AFFILIATIONS
	U. Conn '83	

Lucinda A. Harris, M.D.
505 East 70 St
746-1339

GENERAL OFFICE INFORMATION		HMO/PPO
First Visit:	n/a	
Regular Visit:	n/a	
Accessible:	n/a	
Interpreters:	n/a	
Medicare:	n/a	
Medicaid:	n/a	
Evenings:	n/a	
Saturdays:	n/a	
AmEx:	n/a	
Visa/MC:	n/a	

PATIENT COMMENTS

Pretty thorough and accurate.

Hart, Catherine, M.D.

INFECTIOUS DISEASES · INTERNAL MEDICINE

	DOCTOR	OFFICE	OVERALL
	9.6	8.1	10.0

LANGUAGES	MEDICAL SCHOOL	HOSPITAL AFFILIATIONS
	Univ. of PA '80	NY Hospital-Cornell

72 St. Medical Associates
310 East 72 St
396-3272

GENERAL OFFICE INFORMATION		HMO/PPO
First Visit:	$300	Private Practice
Regular Visit:	$100	
Accessible:	Yes	
Interpreters:	No	
Medicare:	Yes	
Medicaid:	No	
Evenings:	No	
Saturdays:	No	
AmEx:	Yes	
Visa/MC:	Yes	

PATIENT COMMENTS

Absolutely great and I love my doctor.

She is extremely thorough and very patient.

Hauptman, Allen S., M.D.

INTERNAL MEDICINE

DOCTOR	OFFICE	OVERALL
8.5	**7.7**	**8.6**

LANGUAGES	MEDICAL SCHOOL	HOSPITAL AFFILIATIONS
	NYU '78	NYU

Murray Hill Medical Group
317 East 34 St
726-7494

GENERAL OFFICE INFORMATION		HMO/PPO
First Visit:	n/a	Aetna/USH
Regular Visit:	n/a	Chubb
Accessible:	Yes	Oxford
Interpreters:	No	
Medicare:	Yes	
Medicaid:	No	
Evenings:	No	
Saturdays:	No	
AmEx:	Yes	
Visa/MC:	Yes	

PATIENT COMMENTS

This guy is it! Everything you are looking for in a doctor.

Really cares. Really puts a lot of thought into helping you.

He's great! Spends a lot of time and offers good referrals.

Higgins, Lawrence A., D.O., M.P.H.

INTERNAL MEDICINE

DOCTOR	OFFICE	OVERALL
9.0	**9.0**	**9.4**

LANGUAGES	MEDICAL SCHOOL	HOSPITAL AFFILIATIONS
Spanish	NY Osteo, '82	Beth Israel
		Cabrini
		St. Vincent's

Lawrence A. Higgins, DO, MPH
251 West 19 St
741-2330

GENERAL OFFICE INFORMATION		HMO/PPO
First Visit:	$250	Private Practice
Regular Visit:	$85	
Accessible:	Yes	
Interpreters:	No	
Medicare:	Yes	
Medicaid:	No	
Evenings:	Yes	
Saturdays:	No	
AmEx:	Yes	
Visa/MC:	Yes	

PATIENT COMMENTS

Great doctor. I'd refer people to him. At first he wasn't very compassionate, but I like him now.

Hirsch, Lissa, M.D.

GYNECOLOGY

DOCTOR	OFFICE	OVERALL
8.6	**8.9**	**9.1**

LANGUAGES	MEDICAL SCHOOL	HOSPITAL AFFILIATIONS
	UMDNJ '79	Lenox Hill
		NYU

Galasso & Hirsch MD, PC
755 Park Ave
570-2222

GENERAL OFFICE INFORMATION		HMO/PPO
First Visit:	$250	Private Practice
Regular Visit:	$175	
Accessible:	No	
Interpreters:	No	
Medicare:	No	
Medicaid:	No	
Evenings:	No	
Saturdays:	No	
AmEx:	No	
Visa/MC:	Yes	

PATIENT COMMENTS

I feel she provides the best GYN care possible.

Sets a positive example for all doctors.

Ho, Alison, M.D.

				DOCTOR	OFFICE	OVERALL
OB/GYN				**8.3**	**7.1**	**8.8**

LANGUAGES	MEDICAL SCHOOL	HOSPITAL AFFILIATIONS
Spanish	U of PA '82	NYU

Kips Bay OB/GYN, PC
343 East 30 St
679-2213

GENERAL OFFICE INFORMATION		HMO/PPO
First Visit: _____ $200		Chubb
Regular Visit: __ $100		Oxford
Accessible: _____ No		
Interpreters: ____ No		
Medicare: _____ Yes		
Medicaid: _____ No		
Evenings: _____ No		
Saturdays: _____ No		
AmEx: _____ No		
Visa/MC: _____ Yes		

PATIENT COMMENTS

Very good. I was nervous but she calmed me down and told me every step of the way what she was doing.

Others say:

Staff needs a course in telephone manners and wish she would get a new staff.

Hobgood, Laura S., M.D.

				DOCTOR	OFFICE	OVERALL
OB/GYN				**7.8**	**7.1**	**7.4**

LANGUAGES	MEDICAL SCHOOL	HOSPITAL AFFILIATIONS
	Einstein '87	Beth Israel

Laura S Hobgood, MD
137 East 36 St
213-6654

GENERAL OFFICE INFORMATION		HMO/PPO
First Visit: _____ $125		Aetna/USH
Regular Visit: ___ $85		Blue Choice
Accessible: _____ No		PHCS
Interpreters: ____ No		Pru Care
Medicare: _____ Yes		
Medicaid: _____ No		
Evenings: _____ No		
Saturdays: _____ Yes		
AmEx: _____ Yes		
Visa/MC: _____ Yes		

PATIENT COMMENTS

My doctor has provided well for my basic needs but I'm not sure how trustworthy she is. I get the feeling that she's not very experienced in delivering babies and I think she requires frequent visits so that she'll make a profit.

Horbar, Gary, M.D.

				DOCTOR	OFFICE	OVERALL
INTERNAL MEDICINE				**9.1**	**8.7**	**9.5**

LANGUAGES	MEDICAL SCHOOL	HOSPITAL AFFILIATIONS
Spanish	NY Med. '76	Lenox Hill

Horbar, Hochweiss MD, PC
6 East 85 St
570-9119

GENERAL OFFICE INFORMATION		HMO/PPO
First Visit: _____ $150		Healthsource
Regular Visit: __ $100		Oxford
Accessible: _____ Yes		
Interpreters: ____ No		
Medicare: _____ No		
Medicaid: _____ No		
Evenings: _____ No		
Saturdays: _____ No		
AmEx: _____ No		
Visa/MC: _____ Yes		

PATIENT COMMENTS

Good doctor for an intellectual client because he explains processes and reasons behind tests and distracts patients while giving shots

He's very caring, attentive and personable.

Horovitz, H. Leonard, M.D.

INTERNAL MEDICINE · PULMONOLOGY

LANGUAGES	MEDICAL SCHOOL	HOSPITAL AFFILIATIONS
French	NYU '76	Lenox Hill
German		NY Eye & Ear Infirmary

DOCTOR	OFFICE	OVERALL
8.4	7.7	8.3

Leonard H. Horovitz, MD
1065 Park Ave
360-1124

GENERAL OFFICE INFORMATION — **HMO/PPO**

First Visit: _____ n/a
Regular Visit: ___ n/a
Accessible: _____ n/a
Interpreters. ____ n/a
Medicare: _____ n/a
Medicaid: _____ n/a
Evenings: _____ n/a
Saturdays: _____ n/a
AmEx: _____ n/a
Visa/MC: _____ n/a

PATIENT COMMENTS

Personable, knowledgeable and I trust him; and reliable and dynamite!

Horowitz, Mark E., M.D.

FAMILY PRACTICE

LANGUAGES	MEDICAL SCHOOL	HOSPITAL AFFILIATIONS
French	SUNY,	Beth Israel
Spanish	Stony Brook '83	

DOCTOR	OFFICE	OVERALL
6.4	6.8	6.2

Downtown Family Medicine
67 Broad St
482-2400

GENERAL OFFICE INFORMATION — **HMO/PPO**

First Visit: _____ $50 | Aetna/USH
Regular Visit: ___ $50 | Blue Choice
Accessible: _____ Yes | Oxford
Interpreters: ____ No | PHS/Guardian
Medicare: _____ Yes | PHCS
Medicaid: _____ No
Evenings: _____ No
Saturdays: _____ Yes
AmEx: _____ Yes
Visa/MC: _____ Yes

PATIENT COMMENTS

Very overcrowded office. I make appointments with him but always see his associates because he's always busy.

Waited 2 hours one day and never saw him. Phone calls returned in 3 days; appalling.

Hurd, Beverly, M.D.

INTERNAL MEDICINE

LANGUAGES	MEDICAL SCHOOL	HOSPITAL AFFILIATIONS
French	St. Louis Univ. '79	Beth Israel North
		Lenox Hill
		St Luke's-Roosevelt

DOCTOR	OFFICE	OVERALL
7.6	7.9	5.9

Mid Manhattan
Medical Associates
342 East 77 St
734-6620

GENERAL OFFICE INFORMATION — **HMO/PPO**

First Visit: _____ $275 | Aetna/USH
Regular Visit: ___ $85 | Blue Choice
Accessible: _____ No | Cigna
Interpreters: ____ No | Healthsource
Medicare: _____ Yes | PHS/Guardian
Medicaid: _____ No
Evenings: _____ No
Saturdays: _____ No
AmEx: _____ Yes
Visa/MC: _____ No

PATIENT COMMENTS

Jumps to conclusions. Very quick to give me things I don't need.

Isaacs, Daryl M., M.D.

DOCTOR	OFFICE	OVERALL
6.9	8.2	6.6

EMERGENCY MEDICINE · INTERNAL MEDICINE

LANGUAGES	MEDICAL SCHOOL	HOSPITAL AFFILIATIONS
French	Univ. of South	Beth Israel
Hebrew	Africa '80	Downtown
Italian		
Spanish		

Mercer St. Medical
77 Mercer St.
274-0800

GENERAL OFFICE INFORMATION	HMO/PPO
First Visit: _____ $125	Blue Choice
Regular Visit: ___ $90	Chubb
Accessible: _____ No	Oxford
Interpreters: ____ No	PHCS
Medicare: _____ Yes	United Healthcare
Medicaid: _____ No	
Evenings: _____ Yes	
Saturdays: _____ No	
AmEx: _____ Yes	
Visa/MC: _____ Yes	

PATIENT COMMENTS

I wish he were more person-able.

Kabakow, Bernard, M.D.

DOCTOR	OFFICE	OVERALL
6.2	6.8	6.0

INTERNAL MEDICINE · MEDICAL ONCOLOGY

LANGUAGES	MEDICAL SCHOOL	HOSPITAL AFFILIATIONS
Spanish	Vermont '53	Beth Israel
Yiddish		Cabrini
		Manhattan Eye & Ear

Grenville Medical, PC
70 East 10 St
674-4455

GENERAL OFFICE INFORMATION	HMO/PPO
First Visit: _____ $100	Blue Choice
Regular Visit: ___ $60	Chubb
Accessible: _____ Yes	Cigna
Interpreters: ____ No	HealthNet
Medicare: _____ Yes	NYC Care
Medicaid: _____ No	Oxford
Evenings: _____ Yes	PHCS
Saturdays: _____ No	Pru Care
AmEx: _____ No	
Visa/MC: _____ No	

PATIENT COMMENTS

Some say:

he's one of the best, better than Cats!

But others:

feel that he doesn't know his job.

Kadet, Alan, M.D.

DOCTOR	OFFICE	OVERALL
8.9	8.8	9.3

INTERNAL MEDICINE

LANGUAGES	MEDICAL SCHOOL	HOSPITAL AFFILIATIONS
Spanish	Mt. Sinai '81	NY Hospital-Cornell
		St Luke's-Roosevelt

Alan Kadet, MD
65 Central Park West,
Suite 16
721-5600

GENERAL OFFICE INFORMATION	HMO/PPO
First Visit: _____ $125	Aetna/USH
Regular Visit: __ $125	Blue Choice
Accessible: _____ Yes	Cigna
Interpreters: ____ Yes	Local 1199
Medicare: _____ Yes	Local 32BJ
Medicaid: _____ No	PHS/Guardian
Evenings: _____ Yes	United Healthcare
Saturdays: _____ No	
AmEx: _____ Yes	
Visa/MC: _____ Yes	

PATIENT COMMENTS

A great doctor and person-able, energetic, young.

Also intelligent, good about explaining situations in lay terms.

Cares that his patient's under-stand.

Kahn, Max A., M.D.

PEDIATRICS

DOCTOR	OFFICE	OVERALL
8.6	9.0	9.0

LANGUAGES	MEDICAL SCHOOL	HOSPITAL AFFILIATIONS
Albanian	Columbia '75	Lenox Hill
French		NYU
Spanish		St Luke's-Roosevelt

Pediatric & Adolescent
Medicine, LLP
390 West End Ave
787-1444

PATIENT COMMENTS

So far very satisfied; he's very confident and competent.

GENERAL OFFICE INFORMATION	HMO/PPO
First Visit: n/a	Oxford
Regular Visit: n/a	
Accessible: Yes	
Interpreters: No	
Medicare: No	
Medicaid: No	
Evenings: Yes	
Saturdays: Yes	
AmEx: No	
Visa/MC: Yes	

Kamlet, David A., M.D.

GERIATRICS · INTERNAL MEDICINE

DOCTOR	OFFICE	OVERALL
9.2	8.5	9.0

LANGUAGES	MEDICAL SCHOOL	HOSPITAL AFFILIATIONS
Hebrew	'81 Guadelajara,	Beth Israel
Spanish	Mex	Cabrini
		St Luke's-Roosevelt

David A. Kamlet, MD, PC
345 West 58 St
581-4797

PATIENT COMMENTS

He's the best. I recommend him to everyone.

GENERAL OFFICE INFORMATION	HMO/PPO
First Visit: $175	Blue Choice
Regular Visit: $175	HealthNet
Accessible: No	Magna Care
Interpreters: Yes	Multiplan
Medicare: No	Oxford
Medicaid: No	PHCS
Evenings: Yes	Unified
Saturdays: No	United Healthcare
AmEx: Yes	
Visa/MC: Yes	

Kaufman, David L., M.D.

INTERNAL MEDICINE

DOCTOR	OFFICE	OVERALL
8.2	7.8	8.1

LANGUAGES	MEDICAL SCHOOL	HOSPITAL AFFILIATIONS
French	NY Med '77	St. Vincent's
Spanish		

David L Kaufman, MD
314 West 14 St
620-0144

PATIENT COMMENTS

Very business-like, doesn't have much of a personality.

GENERAL OFFICE INFORMATION	HMO/PPO
First Visit: $150	Aetna/USH
Regular Visit: $75	Chubb
Accessible: Yes	Multiplan
Interpreters: No	Oxford
Medicare: Yes	PHS/Guardian
Medicaid: No	PHCS
Evenings: No	Pru Care
Saturdays: No	United Healthcare
AmEx: No	
Visa/MC: No	

Keller, Raymond S., M.D.

INTERNAL MEDICINE · PULMONOLOGY

	DOCTOR	OFFICE	OVERALL
	8.8	7.9	8.3

LANGUAGES	MEDICAL SCHOOL	HOSPITAL AFFILIATIONS
Spanish	NY Med '66	Beth Israel

East Side Physicians, PC
55 East 86 St.
534-1111

GENERAL OFFICE INFORMATION	HMO/PPO
First Visit: _____ $150	Aetna/USH
Regular Visit: __ $150	Blue Choice
Accessible: _____ Yes	Cigna
Interpreters: ____ No	Oxford
Medicare: _____ Yes	PHS/Guardian
Medicaid: _____ No	
Evenings: _____ No	
Saturdays: _____ No	
AmEx: _____ Yes	
Visa/MC: _____ Yes	

PATIENT COMMENTS

He responds quickly and gives advice over the phone.

Kennedy, James T., M.D.

INTERNAL MEDICINE

	DOCTOR	OFFICE	OVERALL
	7.8	6.9	7.2

LANGUAGES	MEDICAL SCHOOL	HOSPITAL AFFILIATIONS
Spanish	NYU '72	NYU

James T. Kennedy, MD
650 First Ave
689-7768

GENERAL OFFICE INFORMATION	HMO/PPO
First Visit: _____ $150	Healthsource
Regular Visit: __ $125	Oxford
Accessible: _____ No	Pru Care
Interpreters: ____ No	
Medicare: _____ No	
Medicaid: _____ No	
Evenings: _____ No	
Saturdays: _____ No	
AmEx: _____ Yes	
Visa/MC: _____ Yes	

PATIENT COMMENTS

Some say:

he's very knowledgeable and they are able to see him promptly.

Other patients say:

the technician is horrible with blood tests and that they provide poor follow-up.

Kennish, Arthur, M.D.

CARDIOLOGY ·· INTERNAL MEDICINE

	DOCTOR	OFFICE	OVERALL
	7.5	7.7	7.6

LANGUAGES	MEDICAL SCHOOL	HOSPITAL AFFILIATIONS
Spanish	Einstein '77	Beth Israel North
		Mount Sinai

Arthur Kennish, MD
108 East 96 St.
410-6610

GENERAL OFFICE INFORMATION	HMO/PPO
First Visit: _____ $175	Aetna/USH
Regular Visit: __ $75	Blue Choice
Accessible: _____ Yes	Chubb
Interpreters: ____ No	Oxford
Medicare: _____ Yes	PHCS
Medicaid: _____ No	Unified
Evenings: _____ No	
Saturdays: _____ No	
AmEx: _____ Yes	
Visa/MC: _____ Yes	

PATIENT COMMENTS

He's not attentive enough.

Lacks compassion, is unreasonable, arrogant and completely ridiculous.

Kessler, Ruth E., M.D.

PEDIATRICS

DOCTOR	OFFICE	OVERALL
7.1	**7.7**	**6.7**

LANGUAGES	MEDICAL SCHOOL	HOSPITAL AFFILIATIONS
German	Marburg, Germany '51	Beth Israel North
		Lenox Hill

Ruth E Kessler, MD
120 East 75 St
734-3338

GENERAL OFFICE INFORMATION	HMO/PPO
First Visit: _____ $150	Aetna/USH
Regular Visit: __ $125	Blue Choice
Accessible: _____ No	Cigna
Interpreters: ____ No	Health Ease
Medicare: _____ No	Independent Health
Medicaid: _____ No	Oxford
Evenings: _____ No	Pru Care
Saturdays: _____ Yes	United Healthcare
AmEx: _____ No	
Visa/MC: _____ No	

PATIENT COMMENTS

If you don't care about personality, she's fine.

I'm not crazy about her.

Khanna, Kussum, M.D.

PEDIATRICS

DOCTOR	OFFICE	OVERALL
8.7	**8.4**	**8.4**

LANGUAGES	MEDICAL SCHOOL	HOSPITAL AFFILIATIONS
Hindi	Dehli Univ.,	Lenox Hill
Spanish	London, '82	St Luke's-Roosevelt

Kussum Khanna, MD
235 West 75 St
496-6440

GENERAL OFFICE INFORMATION	HMO/PPO
First Visit: _____ $125	Aetna/USH
Regular Visit: __ $90	Cigna
Accessible: _____ No	Multiplan
Interpreters: ____ No	Oxford
Medicare: _____ No	PHS/Guardian
Medicaid: _____ No	PHCS
Evenings: _____ Yes	Pru Care
Saturdays: _____ Yes	
AmEx: _____ No	
Visa/MC: _____ No	

PATIENT COMMENTS

Some say:

*he's an excellent doctor;
highly recommended.*

But others say:

*he's hasty, and doesn't let you
get a word in.*

Klein, Susan, M.D.

INTERNAL MEDICINE

DOCTOR	OFFICE	OVERALL
7.2	**7.8**	**7.7**

LANGUAGES	MEDICAL SCHOOL	HOSPITAL AFFILIATIONS
Hungarian	Budapest, Hung '76	Beth Israel North
Tagalog		

Susan E. Klein, MD
120 East 79 St
861-0400

GENERAL OFFICE INFORMATION	HMO/PPO
First Visit: _____ $165	Aetna/USH
Regular Visit: ___ n/a	Blue Choice
Accessible: _____ Yes	Cigna
Interpreters: ____ No	NYC Care
Medicare: _____ Yes	Oxford
Medicaid: _____ No	PHCS
Evenings: _____ No	United Healthcare
Saturdays: _____ No	
AmEx: _____ No	
Visa/MC: _____ No	

PATIENT COMMENTS

Sweet, nice bedside manner.

*I felt very comfortable seeing
her.*

Kling, Alan R., M.D.

DERMATOLOGY

	DOCTOR	OFFICE	OVERALL
	7.8	8.0	7.6

LANGUAGES	MEDICAL SCHOOL	HOSPITAL AFFILIATIONS
French	Emory '78	Beth Israel
Spanish		Mount Sinai

Alan R Kling, MD
1000 Park Ave
288-1300

GENERAL OFFICE INFORMATION	HMO/PPO
First Visit: _____ $125	Aetna/USH
Regular Visit: ___ $95	Affordable Network
Accessible: _____ Yes	Chubb
Interpreters: ____ No	Local 32BJ
Medicare: _____ Yes	Magna Care
Medicaid: _____ No	Oxford
Evenings: _____ Yes	PHS/Guardian
Saturdays: _____ No	PHCS
AmEx: _____ No	
Visa/MC: _____ Yes	

PATIENT COMMENTS

Likes to tell long stories but a good person.

Konecky, Alan, M.D.

CRITICAL CARE · INTERNAL MEDICINE · PULMONOLOGY

	DOCTOR	OFFICE	OVERALL
	8.5	8.6	8.8

LANGUAGES	MEDICAL SCHOOL	HOSPITAL AFFILIATIONS
Cantonese	Columbia '83	Lenox Hill
Mandarin		
Spanish		

Alan Konecky, MD
178 East 85 St.
861-6885

GENERAL OFFICE INFORMATION	HMO/PPO
First Visit: _____ $150	Blue Choice
Regular Visit: __ $125	Chubb
Accessible: _____ Yes	Cigna
Interpreters: ____ No	Health Ease
Medicare: _____ Yes	Oxford
Medicaid: _____ No	PHS/Guardian
Evenings: _____ No	Pru Care
Saturdays: _____ No	United Healthcare
AmEx: _____ Yes	
Visa/MC: _____ Yes	

PATIENT COMMENTS

Smart guy, professional, can explain things well to patients yet his office needs an interior decorator.

And, good guy—great doctor. Good diagnostician.

Kramer, Sara, M.D.

INTERNAL MEDICINE · RHEUMATOLOGY

	DOCTOR	OFFICE	OVERALL
	7.4	7.7	7.8

LANGUAGES	MEDICAL SCHOOL	HOSPITAL AFFILIATIONS
Spanish	SUNY, B'klyn '78	Joint Diseases
		NYU

Sara Kramer, MD
436 Third Ave
889-3911

GENERAL OFFICE INFORMATION	HMO/PPO
First Visit: _____ $350	Aetna/USH
Regular Visit: __ $125	Blue Choice
Accessible: _____ Yes	Cigna
Interpreters: ____ No	Healthsource
Medicare: _____ No	Oxford
Medicaid: _____ No	PHS/Guardian
Evenings: _____ No	Pru Care
Saturdays: _____ No	United Healthcare
AmEx: _____ Yes	
Visa/MC: _____ Yes	

PATIENT COMMENTS

Difficult to get appointments and hard to get referrals.

Lamm, Steven, M.D.

INTERNAL MEDICINE	DOCTOR	OFFICE	OVERALL
	6.8	6.7	7.0

LANGUAGES	MEDICAL SCHOOL	HOSPITAL AFFILIATIONS
German	NYU '74	Lenox Hill
Italian		NYU
Polish		
Spanish		

Steven Lamm, MD
12 East 86 St.
988-1146

GENERAL OFFICE INFORMATION	HMO/PPO
First Visit: _____ $200	Affordable Network
Regular Visit: ___ $75	Chubb
Accessible: _____ No	Multiplan
Interpreters: ____ No	Oxford
Medicare: _____ No	United Healthcare
Medicaid: _____ No	
Evenings: _____ No	
Saturdays: _____ No	
AmEx: _____ No	
Visa/MC: _____ Yes	

PATIENT COMMENTS

Very poorly managed practice. He cares more about himself than his patients.

You often see him on television, that's why people sit and wait for him for hours before they can be seen.

Langelier, Carolyn A., M.D.

INTERNAL MEDICINE	DOCTOR	OFFICE	OVERALL
	8.6	8.6	8.6

LANGUAGES	MEDICAL SCHOOL	HOSPITAL AFFILIATIONS
Portugese	Cornell '89	NYU
Spanish		

Muray Hill Medical Group
317 East 34 St
726-7424

GENERAL OFFICE INFORMATION	HMO/PPO
First Visit: _____ $260	
Regular Visit: __ $125	
Accessible: _____ Yes	
Interpreters: ____ No	
Medicare: _____ Yes	
Medicaid: _____ No	
Evenings: _____ Yes	
Saturdays: _____ No	
AmEx: _____ Yes	
Visa/MC: _____ Yes	

PATIENT COMMENTS

Very personable, with a good bedside manner.

Lantz, Howard, M.D.

PEDIATRICS	DOCTOR	OFFICE	OVERALL
	7.7	6.7	7.0

LANGUAGES	MEDICAL SCHOOL	HOSPITAL AFFILIATIONS
Spanish	NY Med. '70	Beth Israel
		Lenox Hill

Howard Lantz, MD
215 East 95 St.
423-3440

GENERAL OFFICE INFORMATION	HMO/PPO
First Visit: _____ $80	Private Practice
Regular Visit: ___ $60	
Accessible: _____ Yes	
Interpreters: ____ No	
Medicare: _____ No	
Medicaid: _____ No	
Evenings: _____ Yes	
Saturdays: _____ Yes	
AmEx: _____ No	
Visa/MC: _____ Yes	

PATIENT COMMENTS

Basically good.

Larson, Carol, M.D.

DOCTOR	OFFICE	OVERALL
7.9	7.8	8.1

INTERNAL MEDICINE

LANGUAGES	MEDICAL SCHOOL	HOSPITAL AFFILIATIONS
	U. Conn. '82	St Luke's-Roosevelt

West Park Medical
50 West 77 St
247-8100

GENERAL OFFICE INFORMATION	HMO/PPO
First Visit: _____ n/a	
Regular Visit: ___ n/a	
Accessible: _____ n/a	
Interpreters: ____ n/a	
Medicare: _____ n/a	
Medicaid: _____ n/a	
Evenings: _____ n/a	
Saturdays: _____ n/a	
AmEx: _____ n/a	
Visa/MC: _____ n/a	

PATIENT COMMENTS

Some say:

she does her job well and doesn't rush anything.

Others say:

A little cold and no bedside manner. Not very communicative.

Lazarus, Herbert, M.D.

DOCTOR	OFFICE	OVERALL
8.6	8.8	9.2

PEDIATRIC ALLERGY · PEDIATRIC RHEUMATOLOGY · PEDIATRICS

LANGUAGES	MEDICAL SCHOOL	HOSPITAL AFFILIATIONS
French	UMDNJ '83	Bellevue
Spanish		Lenox Hill
		NYU
		St Luke's-Roosevelt

Pediatiric & Adolescent Medicine, LLP
390 West End Ave
787-1444

GENERAL OFFICE INFORMATION	HMO/PPO
First Visit: _____$120	Oxford
Regular Visit: ___$90	
Accessible: _____ Yes	
Interpreters: ____ No	
Medicare: _____ No	
Medicaid: _____ No	
Evenings: _____ Yes	
Saturdays: _____ Yes	
AmEx: _____ No	
Visa/MC: _____ Yes	

PATIENT COMMENTS

Very late for appointments but I love and adore him.

Lebowitz, Nancy, M.D.

DOCTOR	OFFICE	OVERALL
7.7	8.1	7.7

OB/GYN

LANGUAGES	MEDICAL SCHOOL	HOSPITAL AFFILIATIONS
Spanish	Cincinnati '82	NY Hospital-Cornell

Nancy Lebowitz, MD, PC
121 East 69 St.
472-8676

GENERAL OFFICE INFORMATION	HMO/PPO
First Visit: _____$225	Oxford
Regular Visit: __$200	PHCS
Accessible: _____ No	United Healthcare
Interpreters: ____ No	
Medicare: _____ No	
Medicaid: _____ No	
Evenings: _____ No	
Saturdays: _____ No	
AmEx: _____ Yes	
Visa/MC: _____ Yes	

PATIENT COMMENTS

I wasn't happy with her.

Leeds, Gary, M.D.

DOCTOR	OFFICE	OVERALL
7.7	**6.8**	**6.9**

FAMILY PRACTICE

LANGUAGES	MEDICAL SCHOOL	HOSPITAL AFFILIATIONS
Portugese	Brown Univ. '78	Beth Israel
Spanish		Cabrini

Family Medical Group
77 West 15 St
206-7717

GENERAL OFFICE INFORMATION	HMO/PPO
First Visit: _____ $90	Aetna/USH
Regular Visit: ___ $55	Blue Choice
Accessible: _____ Yes	Cigna
Interpreters: ____ No	NYC Care
Medicare: _____ Yes	Oxford
Medicaid: _____ No	
Evenings: _____ No	
Saturdays: _____ No	
AmEx: _____ No	
Visa/MC: _____ No	

PATIENT COMMENTS

Cannot get in touch on the phone and basic feeling of mistrust.

Too many patients and no special attention

Leichman, Gerald, M.D.

DOCTOR	OFFICE	OVERALL
7.8	**6.3**	**7.4**

FAMILY PRACTICE

LANGUAGES	MEDICAL SCHOOL	HOSPITAL AFFILIATIONS
Russian	Guadalajara, Mex '75	Beth Israel
Spanish		

Docs at 34 St.
55 East 34 St.
252-6000

GENERAL OFFICE INFORMATION	HMO/PPO
First Visit: _____ n/a	Aetna/USH
Regular Visit: ___ n/a	Oxford
Accessible: _____ Yes	
Interpreters: ____ No	
Medicare: _____ Yes	
Medicaid: _____ No	
Evenings: _____ Yes	
Saturdays: _____ Yes	
AmEx: _____ Yes	
Visa/MC: _____ Yes	

PATIENT COMMENTS

The phone system is horrible. Care is good.

Leventhal, Gerald H., M.D.

DOCTOR	OFFICE	OVERALL
8.8	**8.4**	**8.7**

INTERNAL MEDICINE · RHEUMATOLOGY

LANGUAGES	MEDICAL SCHOOL	HOSPITAL AFFILIATIONS
	SUNY, B'klyn '64	Beth Israel
		Joint Diseases
		Lenox Hill

Gerald H Leventhal, MD
1020 Park Ave
861-6031

GENERAL OFFICE INFORMATION	HMO/PPO
First Visit: _____ $225	Aetna/USH
Regular Visit: ___ $95	Oxford
Accessible: _____ Yes	Pru Care
Interpreters: ____ No	United Healthcare
Medicare: _____ No	
Medicaid: _____ No	
Evenings: _____ No	
Saturdays: _____ No	
AmEx: _____ No	
Visa/MC: _____ No	

PATIENT COMMENTS

Levine, Susan, M.D.

ALLERGY & IMMULOGY · INFECTIOUS DISEASES · INTERNAL MEDICINE

DOCTOR	OFFICE	OVERALL
6.2	6.3	5.1

LANGUAGES	MEDICAL SCHOOL	HOSPITAL AFFILIATIONS
Spanish	Einstein '81	Beth Israel North

Susan Levine, MD
889 Lexington Ave
472-4816

PATIENT COMMENTS

GENERAL OFFICE INFORMATION	HMO/PPO
First Visit: _____ n/a	Aetna/USH
Regular Visit: ___ n/a	Oxford
Accessible: _____ Yes	PHS/Guardian
Interpreters: ____ No	
Medicare: _____ Yes	
Medicaid: _____ No	
Evenings: _____ Yes	
Saturdays: _____ No	
AmEx: _____ No	
Visa/MC: _____ No	

She's easy to get referrals from, but she doesn't spend too much time with you

She's usually picked based on location and convenience but she's horrible really.

Levy, Albert, M.D.

FAMILY PRACTICE · GERIATRICS

DOCTOR	OFFICE	OVERALL
7.9	8.0	8.0

LANGUAGES	MEDICAL SCHOOL	HOSPITAL AFFILIATIONS
French	Univ. of Brazil '73	Beth Israel North
Portugese		Lenox Hill
Spanish		St Luke's-Roosevelt

Manhattan Family Practice
911 Park Ave
288-7193

PATIENT COMMENTS

GENERAL OFFICE INFORMATION	HMO/PPO
First Visit: _____ n/a	Aetna/USH
Regular Visit: ___ n/a	Chubb
Accessible: _____ No	Cigna
Interpreters: ____ No	Oxford
Medicare: _____ Yes	Pru Care
Medicaid: _____ No	United Healthcare
Evenings: _____ No	
Saturdays: _____ Yes	
AmEx: _____ Yes	
Visa/MC: _____ Yes	

Always spends the extra time. but he's extremely expensive.

Pushes hard to make you take many expensive tests.

Lewin, Margaret, M.D.

HEMATOLOGY · INTERNAL MEDICINE · MEDICAL ONCOLOGY

DOCTOR	OFFICE	OVERALL
8.6	8.7	8.7

LANGUAGES	MEDICAL SCHOOL	HOSPITAL AFFILIATIONS
	Western Reserve '77	Lenox Hill
		NY Hospital-Cornell
		St Luke's-Roosevelt

Manhattan Medical Assoc.
114 East 72 St
737-7910

PATIENT COMMENTS

GENERAL OFFICE INFORMATION	HMO/PPO
First Visit: _____ $175	Cigna
Regular Visit: __ $135	Oxford
Accessible: _____ Yes	PHS/Guardian
Interpreters: ____ No	
Medicare: _____ Yes	
Medicaid: _____ No	
Evenings: _____ No	
Saturdays: _____ No	
AmEx: _____ Yes	
Visa/MC: _____ Yes	

A thorough and highly competent physician.

Lewin, Neal A., M.D.

EMERGENCY MEDICINE · INTERNAL MEDICINE

DOCTOR	OFFICE	OVERALL
8.9	**8.1**	**9.0**

LANGUAGES	MEDICAL SCHOOL	HOSPITAL AFFILIATIONS
French	SUNY, Bklyn '74	Bellevue
Spanish		NYU

Neal A Lewin, MD
120 East 36 St
889-2813

GENERAL OFFICE INFORMATION	HMO/PPO
First Visit: _____ $250	Chubb
Regular Visit: ___ n/a	Oxford
Accessible: _____ Yes	
Interpreters: ____ Yes	
Medicare: _____ No	
Medicaid: _____ No	
Evenings: _____ No	
Saturdays: _____ No	
AmEx: _____ Yes	
Visa/MC: _____ Yes	

PATIENT COMMENTS

Provides excellent, prompt and attentive service. I have full confidence in his abilities. I love this guy. He always takes my calls when I am sick. Very accessible.

Lichtenfeld, Amy D., M.D.

ALLERGY & IMMULOGY · INTERNAL MEDICINE

DOCTOR	OFFICE	OVERALL
7.2	**7.4**	**7.2**

LANGUAGES	MEDICAL SCHOOL	HOSPITAL AFFILIATIONS
Spanish	Univ. PA '84	Beth Israel North
		Lenox Hill
		NY Hospital-Cornell

Amy D Lichtenfeld, MD
178 East 85 St
288-2278

GENERAL OFFICE INFORMATION	HMO/PPO
First Visit: _____ $250	Aetna/USH
Regular Visit: ___ $95	Blue Choice
Accessible: _____ Yes	Cigna
Interpreters: ____ No	Oxford
Medicare: _____ Yes	Pru Care
Medicaid: _____ No	United Healthcare
Evenings: _____ No	
Saturdays: _____ No	
AmEx: _____ Yes	
Visa/MC: _____ No	

PATIENT COMMENTS

Livoti, Carol, M.D.

OB/GYN

DOCTOR	OFFICE	OVERALL
9.1	**9.4**	**9.7**

LANGUAGES	MEDICAL SCHOOL	HOSPITAL AFFILIATIONS
Arabic	NY Med '68	Lenox Hill
French		
Spanish		

Livoti, Sassoon & Sillay
MD, PC
266 East 78 St
288-1669

GENERAL OFFICE INFORMATION	HMO/PPO
First Visit: _____ $200	Private Practice
Regular Visit: __ $170	
Accessible: _____ Yes	
Interpreters: ____ No	
Medicare: _____ No	
Medicaid: _____ No	
Evenings: _____ Yes	
Saturdays: _____ No	
AmEx: _____ Yes	
Visa/MC: _____ Yes	

PATIENT COMMENTS

A credit to her profession.

Pleasant, efficient, as much time as you need but doesn't waste your time.

Great personality, makes you feel comfortable; and worth the wait . . . She is the best doctor in the world and I trust her on every level.

Long, Willam T., Dr.

DERMATOLOGY

LANGUAGES	MEDICAL SCHOOL	HOSPITAL AFFILIATIONS
	Georgetown '82	

DOCTOR	OFFICE	OVERALL
8.9	8.9	9.2

Dr. William T. Long
71 Park Ave
689-9587

GENERAL OFFICE INFORMATION	HMO/PPO
First Visit: _____ n/a	
Regular Visit: ___ n/a	
Accessible: _____ n/a	
Interpreters: ____ n/a	
Medicare: _____ n/a	
Medicaid: _____ n/a	
Evenings: _____ n/a	
Saturdays: _____ n/a	
AmEx: _____ n/a	
Visa/MC: _____ n/a	

PATIENT COMMENTS

Loria, Jeffrey M., M.D.

GASTROENTEROLOGY · INTERNAL MEDICINE

LANGUAGES	MEDICAL SCHOOL	HOSPITAL AFFILIATIONS
Spanish	NY Med '87	Beth Israel North
		Lenox Hill

DOCTOR	OFFICE	OVERALL
8.2	8.6	6.4

Jeffrey M Loria, MD
19 East 80 St
288-2278

GENERAL OFFICE INFORMATION	HMO/PPO
First Visit: _____ $200	Aetna/USH
Regular Visit: ___ $85	Chubb
Accessible: _____ Yes	Cigna
Interpreters: ____ No	Oxford
Medicare: _____ Yes	PHS/Guardian
Medicaid: _____ No	PHCS
Evenings: _____ Yes	Pru Care
Saturdays: _____ No	United Healthcare
AmEx: _____ Yes	
Visa/MC: _____ No	

PATIENT COMMENTS

Effective, but does not have a good bedside manner.

Lustbader, Ian, M.D.

GASTROENTEROLOGY · INTERNAL MEDICINE

LANGUAGES	MEDICAL SCHOOL	HOSPITAL AFFILIATIONS
Spanish	Columbia '82	NYU

DOCTOR	OFFICE	OVERALL
7.7	7.0	7.3

Ian Lustbader, MD
245 East 35 St
685-5252

GENERAL OFFICE INFORMATION	HMO/PPO
First Visit: _____ $300	Blue Choice
Regular Visit: __ $100	GHI
Accessible: _____ No	Healthsource
Interpreters: ____ No	Oxford
Medicare: _____ Yes	United Healthcare
Medicaid: _____ No	
Evenings: _____ Yes	
Saturdays: _____ No	
AmEx: _____ Yes	
Visa/MC: _____ No	

PATIENT COMMENTS

Made some comments which made me very uncomfortable.

I didn't feel that everything would be held in confidence.

Lutsky, Eric, D.O.

DOCTOR	OFFICE	OVERALL
7.6	**8.2**	**8.8**

INTERNAL MEDICINE

LANGUAGES	MEDICAL SCHOOL	HOSPITAL AFFILIATIONS
Spanish	NY Coll of Osteo '89	Beth Israel
		Cabrini

Madison Ave. Medical
Practice
213 Madison Ave.
686-6622

PATIENT COMMENTS

GENERAL OFFICE INFORMATION	HMO/PPO
First Visit: _____ $185	Aetna/USH
Regular Visit: ___ $75	Anthem Health
Accessible: _____ Yes	Blue Choice
Interpreters: ____ No	Cigna
Medicare: _____ Yes	Local 32BJ
Medicaid: _____ No	Multiplan
Evenings: _____ No	Oxford
Saturdays: _____ No	PHCS
AmEx: _____ No	
Visa/MC: _____ No	

Manos, Ellen, M.D.

DOCTOR	OFFICE	OVERALL
8.5	**8.5**	**8.5**

OB/GYN

LANGUAGES	MEDICAL SCHOOL	HOSPITAL AFFILIATIONS
	SUNY, Syracuse '82	Lenox Hill
		St Luke's-Roosevelt

Manos & Ahgharian, MD PC
125 East 63 St
759-6623

PATIENT COMMENTS

GENERAL OFFICE INFORMATION	HMO/PPO
First Visit: _____ $185	Private Practice
Regular Visit: __ $160	
Accessible: _____ Yes	
Interpreters: ____ No	
Medicare: _____ No	
Medicaid: _____ No	
Evenings: _____ No	
Saturdays: _____ No	
AmEx: _____ No	
Visa/MC: _____ Yes	

Some say:

*been a patient for 7 years—
no complaints whatsoever.*

But others say:

*I would not recommend her,
she's a total rip-off and wish
that fees would be explained
in advance.*

Mattes, Leonard, M.D.

DOCTOR	OFFICE	OVERALL
8.7	**7.7**	**9.0**

CARDIOLOGY · INTERNAL MEDICINE

LANGUAGES	MEDICAL SCHOOL	HOSPITAL AFFILIATIONS
Spanish	Tulane '62	Mount Sinai

Mattes & Bergman, MD PC
1199 Park Ave
876-7045

PATIENT COMMENTS

*He asks questions and is
thoughtful and personable.*

A good GP who isn't arrogant.

*He makes you feel like an
equal.*

GENERAL OFFICE INFORMATION	HMO/PPO
First Visit: _____ $250	Aetna/USH
Regular Visit: __ $125	Blue Choice
Accessible: _____ Yes	Health Ease
Interpreters: ____ No	HealthNet
Medicare: _____ Yes	Oxford
Medicaid: _____ No	
Evenings: _____ No	
Saturdays: _____ No	
AmEx: _____ Yes	
Visa/MC: _____ Yes	

Mellow, Nancy L., M.D.

DOCTOR	OFFICE	OVERALL
8.9	8.7	9.3

INTERNAL MEDICINE

LANGUAGES	MEDICAL SCHOOL	HOSPITAL AFFILIATIONS
French	Columbia '77	St. Vincent's
Spanish		

Nancy L. Mellow, MD
88 University Pl
242-0430

GENERAL OFFICE INFORMATION	HMO/PPO
First Visit: _____ $275	Multiplan
Regular Visit: __ $175	
Accessible: _____ No	
Interpreters: ____ No	
Medicare: _____ No	
Medicaid: _____ No	
Evenings: _____ Yes	
Saturdays: _____ No	
AmEx: _____ No	
Visa/MC: _____ No	

PATIENT COMMENTS

*Very nice and easy-going.
Detailed and attentive.*

Merker, Edward, M.D.

DOCTOR	OFFICE	OVERALL
8.6	8.6	9.0

ENDOCRINOLOGY · INTERNAL MEDICINE

LANGUAGES	MEDICAL SCHOOL	HOSPITAL AFFILIATIONS
Romanian	NYU '65	Cabrini
Spanish		Lenox Hill
		Mount Sinai

Edward Merker, MD
35 East 85 St
288-1110

GENERAL OFFICE INFORMATION	HMO/PPO
First Visit: _____ $150	Aetna/USH
Regular Visit: __ $85	Blue Choice
Accessible: _____ No	Oxford
Interpreters: ____ No	
Medicare: _____ Yes	
Medicaid: _____ No	
Evenings: _____ Yes	
Saturdays: _____ No	
AmEx: _____ No	
Visa/MC: _____ Yes	

PATIENT COMMENTS

*The best I've ever had, really
personable and attentive to
your needs.*

Others say:

he's good but busy.

Mernick, Mitchel, M.D.

DOCTOR	OFFICE	OVERALL
6.6	6.1	6.7

GERIATRICS · INTERNAL MEDICINE · MEDICAL ONCOLOGY

LANGUAGES	MEDICAL SCHOOL	HOSPITAL AFFILIATIONS
Hebrew	Mt. Sinai, NY '82	Beth Israel
Russian		Cabrini
Spanish		Joint Diseases
Yiddish		

Park Ave. Medical &
Nutrition, PC
15 Park Ave
686-0901

GENERAL OFFICE INFORMATION	HMO/PPO
First Visit: _____ $200	Aetna/USH
Regular Visit: __ $90	Anthem Health
Accessible: _____ Yes	Blue Choice
Interpreters: ____ Yes	Cigna
Medicare: _____ Yes	Independent Health
Medicaid: _____ No	Oxford
Evenings: _____ Yes	PHS/Guardian
Saturdays: _____ Yes	United Healthcare
AmEx: _____ Yes	
Visa/MC: _____ Yes	

PATIENT COMMENTS

*He has two offices on Park
Ave separated by an apart-
ment building and runs from
one to the other.*

Problematic service.

Overbooking is abominable.

Montana, John, M.D.

DOCTOR	OFFICE	OVERALL
7.6	7.2	6.9

INTERNAL MEDICINE · INFECTIOUS DISEASES

LANGUAGES	MEDICAL SCHOOL	HOSPITAL AFFILIATIONS
Spanish	NY Med. '79	Cabrini

John Montana, MD
30 Fifth Ave
979-8552

GENERAL OFFICE INFORMATION		HMO/PPO
First Visit:	$150	Aetna/USH
Regular Visit:	$75	Blue Choice
Accessible:	Yes	NYC Care
Interpreters:	Yes	
Medicare:	Yes	
Medicaid:	Yes	
Evenings:	Yes	
Saturdays:	No	
AmEx:	No	
Visa/MC:	Yes	

PATIENT COMMENTS

Patients say there's room for improvement.

The doctor is overworked and doesn't allow adequate time for appointments.

Moyer, Lawson, M.D.

DOCTOR	OFFICE	OVERALL
9.6	9.5	9.7

INTERNAL MEDICINE

LANGUAGES	MEDICAL SCHOOL	HOSPITAL AFFILIATIONS
	Virginia '72	NY Hospital-Cornell

Lawson Moyer, MD
955 Lexington Ave
288-4638

GENERAL OFFICE INFORMATION		HMO/PPO
First Visit:	$180	Aetna/USH
Regular Visit:	$65	Anthem Health
Accessible:	Yes	Blue Choice
Interpreters:	No	Oxford
Medicare:	No	United Healthcare
Medicaid:	No	
Evenings:	No	
Saturdays:	No	
AmEx:	No	
Visa/MC:	No	

PATIENT COMMENTS

Very personable and easy to talk to.

Very good at answering questions. I really trust him.

He's conscientious, reliable, and goes the extra mile for his patients.

Mueller, Richard L., M.D.

DOCTOR	OFFICE	OVERALL
7.3	5.8	7.2

CARDIOLOGY · INTERNAL MEDICINE

LANGUAGES	MEDICAL SCHOOL	HOSPITAL AFFILIATIONS
Greek	UC San Francisco '87	NY Hospital-Cornell
Hungarian		St Luke's-Roosevelt
Spanish		

Medical Associates of NY
133 East 58 St #909
593-9800

GENERAL OFFICE INFORMATION		HMO/PPO
First Visit:	$175	Aetna/USH
Regular Visit:	$70	Blue Choice
Accessible:	Yes	Cigna
Interpreters:	No	Local 32BJ
Medicare:	Yes	Oxford
Medicaid:	No	PHS/Guardian
Evenings:	Yes	United Healthcare
Saturdays:	Yes .	
AmEx:	Yes	
Visa/MC:	Yes	

PATIENT COMMENTS

Mediocre and always seems rushed.

I would be more inclined to see this doctor if his staff were more efficient.

Murphy, Ramon J. C., M.D.

DOCTOR	OFFICE	OVERALL
8.6	**8.3**	**9.3**

PEDIATRICS

LANGUAGES	MEDICAL SCHOOL	HOSPITAL AFFILIATIONS
Spanish	Northwestern '69	Mount Sinai

Uptown Pediatrics
1175 Park Ave
427-0540

GENERAL OFFICE INFORMATION	HMO/PPO
First Visit: _____ $150	Private Practice
Regular Visit: ___ $85	
Accessible: _____ Yes	
Interpreters: ____ No	
Medicare: _____ No	
Medicaid: _____ No	
Evenings: _____ Yes	
Saturdays: _____ Yes	
AmEx: _____ Yes	
Visa/MC: _____ Yes	

PATIENT COMMENTS

Some say:
excellent doctor.
Very warm and kind.
But others say:
he needs to work on his phone skills.

Nachamie, Rebecca, M.D.

DOCTOR	OFFICE	OVERALL
8.4	**8.3**	**8.5**

OB/GYN

LANGUAGES	MEDICAL SCHOOL	HOSPITAL AFFILIATIONS
Italian	SUNY, Albany '69	Mount Sinai
Polish		
Spanish		

Nachamie, Bello, Callipari
47 East 88 St
996-9800

GENERAL OFFICE INFORMATION	HMO/PPO
First Visit: _____ $230	Oxford
Regular Visit: __ $190	
Accessible: _____ Yes	
Interpreters: ____ Yes	
Medicare: _____ No	
Medicaid: _____ No	
Evenings: _____ Yes	
Saturdays: _____ Yes	
AmEx: _____ Yes	
Visa/MC: _____ Yes	

PATIENT COMMENTS

A credit to her profession but always late.
It takes a long time to make an appointment except in emergencies.

Nadel, Lester, M.D.

DOCTOR	OFFICE	OVERALL
7.4	**7.9**	**7.5**

INTERNAL MEDICINE

LANGUAGES	MEDICAL SCHOOL	HOSPITAL AFFILIATIONS
Spanish	NYU '74	Beth Israel
		Cabrini
		St. Vincent's

Lester Nadel, MD
235 East 22 St
697-2585

GENERAL OFFICE INFORMATION	HMO/PPO
First Visit: _____ $100	Aetna/USH
Regular Visit: ___ n/a	Cigna
Accessible: _____ No	Local 32BJ
Interpreters: ____ No	Magna Care
Medicare: _____ Yes	Oxford
Medicaid: _____ No	PHCS
Evenings: _____ No	United Healthcare
Saturdays: _____ No	
AmEx: _____ No	
Visa/MC: _____ No	

PATIENT COMMENTS

Professional and knowledgeable.

Nash, Thomas W., M.D.

INFECTIOUS DISEASES · INTERNAL MEDICINE · PULMONOLOGY

DOCTOR	OFFICE	OVERALL
9.1	9.3	9.4

LANGUAGES	MEDICAL SCHOOL	HOSPITAL AFFILIATIONS
	NYU '78	NY Hospital-Cornell

72 St. Medical Assoc.
310 East 72 St
734-6612

GENERAL OFFICE INFORMATION	HMO/PPO
First Visit: _____ $350	Private Practice
Regular Visit: __ $125	
Accessible: _____ Yes	
Interpreters. ____ No	
Medicare: _____ No	
Medicaid: _____ No	
Evenings: _____ No	
Saturdays: _____ No	
AmEx: _____ Yes	
Visa/MC: _____ Yes	

PATIENT COMMENTS

The best doctor in the city.
A most personable doctor.

Newman, Mark R., M.D.

INTERNAL MEDICINE

DOCTOR	OFFICE	OVERALL
9.3	8.9	9.8

LANGUAGES	MEDICAL SCHOOL	HOSPITAL AFFILIATIONS
	NYU '73	NYU

Mark R. Newman, MD
135 East 37 St
683-7117

GENERAL OFFICE INFORMATION	HMO/PPO
First Visit: _____ n/a	
Regular Visit: ___ n/a	
Accessible: ____ n/a	
Interpreters: ____ n/a	
Medicare: _____ n/a	
Medicaid: _____ n/a	
Evenings: _____ n/a	
Saturdays: _____ n/a	
AmEx: _____ n/a	
Visa/MC: _____ n/a	

PATIENT COMMENTS

A lovely person and a great doctor; personable, caring and very attentive.

Nicolaides, Maria N., M.D.

INTERNAL MEDICINE · NEPHROLOGY

DOCTOR	OFFICE	OVERALL
9.1	8.8	9.2

LANGUAGES	MEDICAL SCHOOL	HOSPITAL AFFILIATIONS
Greek	Columbia '87	Columbia Presbyterian
Spanish		

Maria N. Nicolaides, MD
903 Park Ave.
327-4382

GENERAL OFFICE INFORMATION	HMO/PPO
First Visit: _____ $375	Aetna/USH
Regular Visit: ___ n/a	Blue Choice
Accessible: _____ Yes	Oxford
Interpreters: ____ Yes	PHS/Guardian
Medicare: _____ Yes	PHCS
Medicaid: _____ No	
Evenings: _____ No	
Saturdays: _____ No	
AmEx: _____ Yes	
Visa/MC: _____ Yes	

PATIENT COMMENTS

She's great. Never on time; but when she's with you, she's with you.

Very competent, personable and attentive.

Olmscheid, Bruce, M.D.

FAMILY PRACTICE

DOCTOR	OFFICE	OVERALL
7.6	6.5	8.0

LANGUAGES	MEDICAL SCHOOL	HOSPITAL AFFILIATIONS
Spanish	Univ. Minn '87	St. Vincent's

Medical Associates
of St. Vincent's
32 West 18 St.
604-6463

PATIENT COMMENTS

Satisfactory for an HMO. I wish I got better service though.

GENERAL OFFICE INFORMATION

	HMO/PPO
First Visit: _____ $150	Aetna/USH
Regular Visit: __ $100	Blue Choice
Accessible: _____ Yes	Multiplan
Interpreters: ____ No	Oxford
Medicare: _____ Yes	PHS/Guardian
Medicaid: _____ No	PHCS
Evenings: _____ No	
Saturdays: _____ No	
AmEx: _____ No	
Visa/MC: _____ Yes	

Painter, Lucy N., M.D.

INTERNAL MEDICINE

DOCTOR	OFFICE	OVERALL
8.5	8.5	8.8

LANGUAGES	MEDICAL SCHOOL	HOSPITAL AFFILIATIONS
	St. George's, '86 Grenada	NY Hospital-Cornell

Cornell Medical Associates
130 West 86 St.
758-3590

PATIENT COMMENTS

I like her because he is extremely well-educated and very personable.

Into holistic medicine, doesn't practice it but is up on issues and will research issues to better educate herself and her patients.

GENERAL OFFICE INFORMATION

	HMO/PPO
First Visit: _____ $175	Aetna/USH
Regular Visit: __ $100	Blue Choice
Accessible: _____ Yes	Healthsource
Interpreters: ____ No	NYC Care
Medicare: _____ Yes	Oxford
Medicaid: _____ No	United Healthcare
Evenings: _____ No	
Saturdays: _____ No	
AmEx: _____ Yes	
Visa/MC: _____ Yes	

Palumbo, Michael J., M.D.

INTERNAL MEDICINE

DOCTOR	OFFICE	OVERALL
8.6	7.8	8.7

LANGUAGES	MEDICAL SCHOOL	HOSPITAL AFFILIATIONS
	Boston U. '86	NYU

Murray Hill Medical Group
317 East 34 St
726-7474

PATIENT COMMENTS

Some say:
a rare find in NYC and spends time listening to you.

Others say:
he's terrible with emergencies.

GENERAL OFFICE INFORMATION

	HMO/PPO
First Visit: _____ $250	Aetna/USH
Regular Visit: __ $110	Healthsource
Accessible: _____ Yes	Oxford
Interpreters: ____ No	United Healthcare
Medicare: _____ Yes	
Medicaid: _____ No	
Evenings: _____ Yes	
Saturdays: _____ No	
AmEx: _____ Yes	
Visa/MC: _____ Yes	

Park, Brian, M.D.

OB/GYN

DOCTOR	OFFICE	OVERALL
8.7	8.4	9.4

LANGUAGES	MEDICAL SCHOOL	HOSPITAL AFFILIATIONS
Spanish	Ohio State '89	Beth Israel Lenox Hill

All Womens Health &
Medical Services
184 East 70 St.
650-9191

GENERAL OFFICE INFORMATION	HMO/PPO
First Visit: _____ $175	Cigna
Regular Visit: __ $100	Oxford
Accessible: _____ Yes	PHCS
Interpreters: ____ No	Piu Care
Medicare: _____ No	United Healthcare
Medicaid: _____ No	
Evenings: _____ Yes	
Saturdays: _____ Yes	
AmEx: _____ Yes	
Visa/MC: _____ Yes	

PATIENT COMMENTS

Some say:

very knowledgeable and personable; he cares about his patients well-being.

Others say:

not so friendly—although he seems to know what he's doing.

Park, Constance, M.D.

ENDOCRINOLOGY · INTERNAL MEDICINE

DOCTOR	OFFICE	OVERALL
8.2	6.5	7.5

LANGUAGES	MEDICAL SCHOOL	HOSPITAL AFFILIATIONS
	Einstein '74	Columbia Presbyterian

NY Physicians
635 Madison Ave.
317-4567

GENERAL OFFICE INFORMATION	HMO/PPO
First Visit: _____ $350	Healthsource
Regular Visit: ___ n/a	
Accessible: _____ Yes	
Interpreters: ____ Yes	
Medicare: _____ Yes	
Medicaid: _____ No	
Evenings: _____ No	
Saturdays: _____ No	
AmEx: _____ Yes	
Visa/MC: _____ Yes	

PATIENT COMMENTS

I'm probably going to change.

Pasquariello, Palmo, M.D.

PEDIATRICS

DOCTOR	OFFICE	OVERALL
9.3	8.8	9.2

LANGUAGES	MEDICAL SCHOOL	HOSPITAL AFFILIATIONS
Italian Spanish	NY Med '85	Lenox Hill

Palmo Pasquariello, MD
9 East 68 St
288-0909

GENERAL OFFICE INFORMATION	HMO/PPO
First Visit: _____ $85	Chubb
Regular Visit: __ $85	Oxford
Accessible: _____ Yes	PHCS
Interpreters: ____ No	United Healthcare
Medicare: _____ No	
Medicaid: _____ No	
Evenings: _____ No	
Saturdays: _____ No	
AmEx: _____ No	
Visa/MC: _____ No	

PATIENT COMMENTS

The staff is very courteous and attentive and most importantly respond appropriately to emergencies.

Impeccable; the best; always recommend him for other children.

Pearlman, Kenneth I., M.D.

GASTROENTEROLOGY · INTERNAL MEDICINE

	DOCTOR	OFFICE	OVERALL
	9.0	8.0	8.8

LANGUAGES	MEDICAL SCHOOL	HOSPITAL AFFILIATIONS
	Albany Med. Coll. '83	NYU

Kenneth I. Pearlman, MD
317 East 34 St
726-7444

GENERAL OFFICE INFORMATION	HMO/PPO
First Visit: _____ n/a	Aetna/USH
Regular Visit: ___ n/a	Healthsource
Accessible: _____ Yes	Oxford
Interpreters: ____ No	PHS/Guardian
Medicare: _____ Yes	United Healthcare
Medicaid: _____ No	
Evenings: _____ Yes	
Saturdays: _____ No	
AmEx: _____ Yes	
Visa/MC: _____ Yes	

PATIENT COMMENTS

Very nice guy and caring; always calls.

Pegler, Cynthia, M.D.

ADOLESCENT MEDICINE · PEDIATRICS

	DOCTOR	OFFICE	OVERALL
	8.9	8.5	9.2

LANGUAGES	MEDICAL SCHOOL	HOSPITAL AFFILIATIONS
	Albany Med. College '84	Lenox Hill NY Hospital-Cornell

Cynthia Pegler, MD
418 East 71 St.
772-8989

GENERAL OFFICE INFORMATION	HMO/PPO
First Visit: _____ $300	Private Practice
Regular Visit: ___ $95	
Accessible: _____ Yes	
Interpreters: ____ No	
Medicare: _____ No	
Medicaid: _____ No	
Evenings: _____ Yes	
Saturdays: _____ No	
AmEx: _____ Yes	
Visa/MC: _____ Yes	

PATIENT COMMENTS

She's awesome. She completely understands everything I say.

Really in tune as to what I am going through as a teen.

And, she's the best.

Perskin, Michael, M.D.

INTERNAL MEDICINE

	DOCTOR	OFFICE	OVERALL
	8.4	8.1	8.5

LANGUAGES	MEDICAL SCHOOL	HOSPITAL AFFILIATIONS
Spanish	Brown Univ. '86	Joint Diseases NYU

Concorde Medical Group
135 East 37 St
679-1410

GENERAL OFFICE INFORMATION	HMO/PPO
First Visit: _____ $225	Aetna/USH
Regular Visit: __ $100	Healthsource
Accessible: _____ Yes	Oxford
Interpreters: ____ No	
Medicare: _____ Yes	
Medicaid: _____ No	
Evenings: _____ No	
Saturdays: _____ Yes	
AmEx: _____ Yes	
Visa/MC: _____ Yes	

PATIENT COMMENTS

Good, but a little rushed.

Pitaro, Gregory, M.D.

INTERNAL MEDICINE

DOCTOR	OFFICE	OVERALL
9.6	8.3	9.3

LANGUAGES	MEDICAL SCHOOL	HOSPITAL AFFILIATIONS
	SUNY Downstate '90	Joint Diseases NYU

Murray Hill Medical Group
317 East 34 St.
726-7480

PATIENT COMMENTS

Thorough, personable with a great bedside manner.

GENERAL OFFICE INFORMATION	HMO/PPO
First Visit: _____ n/a	Aetna/USH
Regular Visit: ___ n/a	Chubb
Accessible: _____ Yes	Oxford
Interpreters: ____ No	United Healthcare
Medicare: _____ Yes	
Medicaid: _____ No	
Evenings: _____ Yes	
Saturdays: _____ No	
AmEx: _____ Yes	
Visa/MC: _____ Yes	

Popper, Laura, M.D.

PEDIATRICS

DOCTOR	OFFICE	OVERALL
8.5	8.4	8.9

LANGUAGES	MEDICAL SCHOOL	HOSPITAL AFFILIATIONS
	Columbia '74	Mount Sinai

Laura Popper, MD PC
8 East 77 St
794-2136

PATIENT COMMENTS

Very, very good.

Terrific pediatrician, gives the best shots ever.

Very satisfied.

GENERAL OFFICE INFORMATION	HMO/PPO
First Visit: _____ $125	Private Practice
Regular Visit: ___ $90	
Accessible: _____ No	
Interpreters: ____ No	
Medicare: _____ No	
Medicaid: _____ No	
Evenings: _____ Yes	
Saturdays: _____ Yes	
AmEx: _____ Yes	
Visa/MC: _____ Yes	

Posner, David H., M.D.

CRITICAL CARE · INTERNAL MEDICINE · PULMONOLOGY

DOCTOR	OFFICE	OVERALL
8.9	8.7	9.1

LANGUAGES	MEDICAL SCHOOL	HOSPITAL AFFILIATIONS
Dutch French Italian Spanish	NY Med '81	Beth Israel Lenox Hill

Avenue Medical Associates
178 East 85 St
861-8976

PATIENT COMMENTS

Very personable, efficient, knowledgeable and compassionate.

The best in the city.

GENERAL OFFICE INFORMATION	HMO/PPO
First Visit: _____ $200	Aetna/USH
Regular Visit: __ $100	Blue Choice
Accessible: _____ Yes	Oxford
Interpreters: ____ No	United Healthcare
Medicare: _____ Yes	
Medicaid: _____ No	
Evenings: _____ No	
Saturdays: _____ No	
AmEx: _____ Yes	
Visa/MC: _____ Yes	

Present, Daniel H., M.D.

GASTROENTEROLOGY · INTERNAL MEDICINE

DOCTOR	OFFICE	OVERALL
7.9	**7.9**	**7.6**

LANGUAGES	MEDICAL SCHOOL	HOSPITAL AFFILIATIONS
Spanish	SUNY, Bklyn '59	Mount Sinai

Present & Norman, MD, PC
12 East 86 St
861-2000

GENERAL OFFICE INFORMATION	HMO/PPO
First Visit: _____ $450	Private Practice
Regular Visit: __ $150	
Accessible: _____ Yes	
Interpreters: ____ No	
Medicare: _____ Yes	
Medicaid: _____ No	
Evenings: _____ No	
Saturdays: _____ No	
AmEx: _____ Yes	
Visa/MC: _____ Yes	

PATIENT COMMENTS

Some say:
very friendly and concerned.
Others say:
he wasn't there when it counted.

Radin, Allen, M.D.

INTERNAL MEDICINE · RHEUMATOLOGY

DOCTOR	OFFICE	OVERALL
7.4	**7.3**	**7.4**

LANGUAGES	MEDICAL SCHOOL	HOSPITAL AFFILIATIONS
	NYU '77	Beth Israel North
		Lenox Hill
		NY Hospital-Cornell

Allen Radin, MD
1085 Park Ave
289-6855

GENERAL OFFICE INFORMATION	HMO/PPO
First Visit: _____ $175	Aetna/USH
Regular Visit: __ $125	Blue Choice
Accessible: _____ No	Cigna
Interpreters: ____ No	Healthsource
Medicare: _____ No	Magna Care
Medicaid: _____ No	Oxford
Evenings: _____ No	PHS/Guardian
Saturdays: _____ No	United Healthcare
AmEx: _____ No	
Visa/MC: _____ No	

PATIENT COMMENTS

Some say:
he's great.
Others say:
he doesn't give enough time.

Ravetz, Valerie, M.D.

FAMILY PRACTICE

DOCTOR	OFFICE	OVERALL

LANGUAGES	MEDICAL SCHOOL	HOSPITAL AFFILIATIONS
		St. Vincent's

Riverview Medical Assoc.
51 East 25 St
684-7455

GENERAL OFFICE INFORMATION	HMO/PPO
First Visit: _____ $225	Aetna/USH
Regular Visit: ___ $85	Blue Choice
Accessible: _____ Yes	Multiplan
Interpreters: ____ No	Oxford
Medicare: _____ Yes	PHS/Guardian
Medicaid: _____ No	PHCS
Evenings: _____ Yes	Pru Care
Saturdays: _____ No	
AmEx: _____ Yes	
Visa/MC: _____ Yes	

PATIENT COMMENTS

Very friendly and willing to take the time needed to explain and I like her a lot.

Reiss, Ronald J., M.D.

OB/GYN

	DOCTOR	OFFICE	OVERALL
	8.8	8.6	9.0

LANGUAGES	MEDICAL SCHOOL	HOSPITAL AFFILIATIONS
French	Brussels, Belgium '76	Lenox Hill
Spanish		
Tagalog		

Ronald J. Reiss, MD
124 East 84 St
749-3113

GENERAL OFFICE INFORMATION	HMO/PPO
First Visit: _____ $150	Aetna/USH
Regular Visit: __ $100	Blue Choice
Accessible: _____ No	Chubb
Interpreters: ____ No	Multiplan
Medicare: _____ Yes	Oxford
Medicaid: _____ No	PHS/Guardian
Evenings: _____ No	
Saturdays: _____ No	
AmEx: _____ Yes	
Visa/MC: _____ Yes	

PATIENT COMMENTS

Should be on the list of best doctors is NY and had all the answers before I ever asked.

Rodman, John S., M.D.

INTERNAL MEDICINE · NEPHROLOGY

	DOCTOR	OFFICE	OVERALL
	8.3	7.6	7.6

LANGUAGES	MEDICAL SCHOOL	HOSPITAL AFFILIATIONS
French	Columbia '70	Lenox Hill
Spanish		NY Hospital-Cornell

John S. Rodman, MD
435 East 57 St
752-3043

GENERAL OFFICE INFORMATION	HMO/PPO
First Visit: _____ $300	Private Practice
Regular Visit: __ $125	
Accessible: _____ Yes	
Interpreters: ____ No	
Medicare: _____ No	
Medicaid: _____ No	
Evenings: _____ No	
Saturdays: _____ No	
AmEx: _____ No	
Visa/MC: _____ No	

PATIENT COMMENTS

Rooney, Ellen, M.D.

INTERNAL MEDICINE

	DOCTOR	OFFICE	OVERALL
	9.2	8.2	9.1

LANGUAGES	MEDICAL SCHOOL	HOSPITAL AFFILIATIONS
Spanish	NY Med '83	Lenox Hill

Ellen Rooney, MD
111 East 80 St.
734-5533

GENERAL OFFICE INFORMATION	HMO/PPO
First Visit: _____ n/a	
Regular Visit: ___ n/a	
Accessible: _____ n/a	
Interpreters: ____ n/a	
Medicare: _____ n/a	
Medicaid: _____ n/a	
Evenings: _____ n/a	
Saturdays: _____ n/a	
AmEx: _____ n/a	
Visa/MC: _____ n/a	

PATIENT COMMENTS

Very nice and professional.

I tell my friends to use her as their primary care physician.

She's awesome. Down to earth, easy to talk to.

Rosenbaum, Michael, M.D.

PEDIATRIC ENOCRINOLOGY · PEDIATRICS

	DOCTOR	OFFICE	OVERALL
	8.7	8.1	9.2

LANGUAGES	MEDICAL SCHOOL	HOSPITAL AFFILIATIONS
Spanish	Cornell '82	Lenox Hill NY Hospital-Cornell

West End Pediatrics
450 West End Ave
769-3070

GENERAL OFFICE INFORMATION	HMO/PPO
First Visit: _____ $75	Oxford
Regular Visit: ___ $60	
Accessible: _____ Yes	
Interpreters: ____ No	
Medicare: _____ No	
Medicaid: _____ No	
Evenings: _____ Yes	
Saturdays: _____ Yes	
AmEx: _____ Yes	
Visa/MC: _____ Yes	

PATIENT COMMENTS

Tremendous pediatrician and very easy to talk to.

Rosenfeld, Suzanne, M.D.

PEDIATRICS

	DOCTOR	OFFICE	OVERALL
	8.3	8.2	8.5

LANGUAGES	MEDICAL SCHOOL	HOSPITAL AFFILIATIONS
Spanish	Columbia '80	Lenox Hill NY Hospital-Cornell

West End Pediatrics
450 West End Ave
769-3070

GENERAL OFFICE INFORMATION	HMO/PPO
First Visit: _____ $125	Oxford
Regular Visit: ___ $90	
Accessible: _____ Yes	
Interpreters: ____ No	
Medicare: _____ No	
Medicaid: _____ No	
Evenings: _____ Yes	
Saturdays: _____ Yes	
AmEx: _____ Yes	
Visa/MC: _____ Yes	

PATIENT COMMENTS

She's great at what she does. Excellent physician.

Ruden, Ronald, M.D.

INTERNAL MEDICINE

	DOCTOR	OFFICE	OVERALL
	6.7	6.8	6.9

LANGUAGES	MEDICAL SCHOOL	HOSPITAL AFFILIATIONS
Spanish	Mt. Sinai, NY '75	Beth Israel North Joint Diseases Lenox Hill

Nutrition Associates
121 East 84 St
879-4700

GENERAL OFFICE INFORMATION	HMO/PPO
First Visit: _____ $90	Aetna/USH
Regular Visit: ___ $90	Blue Choice
Accessible: _____ Yes	Chubb
Interpreters: ____ No	Oxford
Medicare: _____ Yes	United Healthcare
Medicaid: _____ No	
Evenings: _____ Yes	
Saturdays: _____ No	
AmEx: _____ Yes	
Visa/MC: _____ Yes	

PATIENT COMMENTS

Keeps you on "hold" forever; staff is incompetent and consider finding someone else.

Rudin, Debra, M.D.

INFECTIOUS DISEASES · INTERNAL MEDICINE

DOCTOR	OFFICE	OVERALL
7.9	7.3	8.0

LANGUAGES	MEDICAL SCHOOL	HOSPITAL AFFILIATIONS
Spanish	Columbia	Columbia Presbyterian

Columbia Presbyterian Eastside
16 East 60 St.
326-8420

GENERAL OFFICE INFORMATION	HMO/PPO
First Visit: _____ $350	
Regular Visit: __ $125	
Accessible: _____ Yes	
Interpreters: ____ No	
Medicare: _____ Yes	
Medicaid: _____ No	
Evenings: _____ Yes	
Saturdays: _____ No	
AmEx: _____ Yes	
Visa/MC: _____ Yes	

PATIENT COMMENTS

Pretty good, but the staff is horrible. They don't even answer the phone.

Sassoon, Albert K., M.D., M.P.H.

OB/GYN

DOCTOR	OFFICE	OVERALL
9.5	9.4	9.6

LANGUAGES	MEDICAL SCHOOL	HOSPITAL AFFILIATIONS
Arabic	NY Med. Coll. '81	Lenox Hill
French		
Spanish		

Livoti, Sassoon, Sillay, MD PC
266 East 78 St
288-1669

GENERAL OFFICE INFORMATION	HMO/PPO
First Visit: _____ $200	Private Practice
Regular Visit: __ $170	
Accessible: _____ Yes	
Interpreters: ____ No	
Medicare: _____ No	
Medicaid: _____ No	
Evenings: _____ Yes	
Saturdays: _____ No	
AmEx: _____ Yes	
Visa/MC: _____ Yes	

PATIENT COMMENTS

Serious, effective physician with obvious concern for patient's safety and well-being.

Very personable and always makes himself available for my questions and concerns.

Couldn't have been better treated. Phenomenal!

Schayes, Bernard, M.D.

GERIATRICS · INTERNAL MEDICINE

DOCTOR	OFFICE	OVERALL
8.1	8.3	8.2

LANGUAGES	MEDICAL SCHOOL	HOSPITAL AFFILIATIONS
French	Bucharest,	Beth Israel
Spanish	Romania '82	Beth Israel North
		Cabrini

Bernard Schayes, MD PC
162 East 80 St.
535-3338

GENERAL OFFICE INFORMATION	HMO/PPO
First Visit: _____ $130	Aetna/USH
Regular Visit: ___ $70	Blue Choice
Accessible: _____ Yes	Cigna
Interpreters: ____ No	NYC Care
Medicare: _____ Yes	
Medicaid: _____ No	
Evenings: _____ No	
Saturdays: _____ No	
AmEx: _____ Yes	
Visa/MC: _____ Yes	

PATIENT COMMENTS

Some say:
nice guy.

But others say:
he prescribes too much medicine and his staff is rude.

Scheiner, Avery M., M.D.

DERMATOLOGY

DOCTOR	OFFICE	OVERALL
9.0	8.8	9.2

Avery Scheiner, MD
156 East 79 St
879-6614

LANGUAGES	MEDICAL SCHOOL	HOSPITAL AFFILIATIONS
	NYU '82	Lenox Hill
		NYU

GENERAL OFFICE INFORMATION	HMO/PPO
First Visit: _____ $150	Aetna/USH
Regular Visit: __ $125	Oxford
Accessible: _____ Yes	PHS/Guardian
Interpreters: ____ No	PHCS
Medicare: _____ Yes	United Healthcare
Medicaid: _____ No	
Evenings: _____ Yes	
Saturdays: _____ No	
AmEx: _____ Yes	
Visa/MC: _____ Yes	

PATIENT COMMENTS

A very talented dermatologist, he takes his time in treatment, explains things and answers questions well.

Schwartz, Lawrence P., M.D.

INTERNAL MEDICINE · PULMONOLOGY

DOCTOR	OFFICE	OVERALL
8.6	8.7	8.6

Lawrence P Schwartz, MD
36 East 38 St
545-7710

LANGUAGES	MEDICAL SCHOOL	HOSPITAL AFFILIATIONS
	NY Med '75	Beth Israel
		Beth Israel North
		Joint Diseases

GENERAL OFFICE INFORMATION	HMO/PPO
First Visit: _____ $150	Aetna/USH
Regular Visit: __ $75	Blue Choice
Accessible: _____ Yes	Oxford
Interpreters: ____ No	PHS/Guardian
Medicare: _____ Yes	United Healthcare
Medicaid: _____ No	
Evenings: _____ No	
Saturdays: _____ No	
AmEx: _____ No	
Visa/MC: _____ No	

PATIENT COMMENTS

Very personable, caring, and easy to talk to and he's a cool guy.

Others say:

too rushed. Should make more time for you.

Schwartz, Stephen, M.D.

PEDIATRICS

DOCTOR	OFFICE	OVERALL
8.6	8.1	8.6

Stephen Schwartz, MD
530 First Ave
263-7220

LANGUAGES	MEDICAL SCHOOL	HOSPITAL AFFILIATIONS
	NYU '68	NYU

GENERAL OFFICE INFORMATION	HMO/PPO
First Visit: _____ $100	
Regular Visit: __ $80	
Accessible: _____ Yes	
Interpreters: ____ No	
Medicare: _____ No	
Medicaid: _____ No	
Evenings: _____ No	
Saturdays: _____ No	
AmEx: _____ No	
Visa/MC: _____ No	

PATIENT COMMENTS

Doctor is fairly good but could be kinder and better.

Seed, Wm., M.D.

PEDIATRICS

	DOCTOR	OFFICE	OVERALL
	7.5	7.4	7.9

LANGUAGES	MEDICAL SCHOOL	HOSPITAL AFFILIATIONS
Spanish	Cornell '62	Lenox Hill NY Hospital-Cornell

William T. Seed, MD PC
56 East 76 St
249-5544

GENERAL OFFICE INFORMATION / **HMO/PPO**

First Visit: _____ $150
Regular Visit: __ $100
Accessible: _____ No
Interpreters: ____ No
Medicare: _____ No
Medicaid: _____ No
Evenings: _____ No
Saturdays: _____ No
AmEx: _____ No
Visa/MC: _____ Yes

Private Practice

PATIENT COMMENTS

Some say:
great.
Another says:
he traumatized me.

Selick, Caryn E., M.D.

OB/GYN

	DOCTOR	OFFICE	OVERALL
	9.1	8.8	9.2

LANGUAGES	MEDICAL SCHOOL	HOSPITAL AFFILIATIONS
	NYU '88	NYU St Luke's-Roosevelt

Caryn E. Selick, MD
338 East 30 St.
683-0090

GENERAL OFFICE INFORMATION / **HMO/PPO**

First Visit: _____ n/a
Regular Visit: __ n/a
Accessible: _____ n/a
Interpreters: ____ n/a
Medicare: _____ n/a
Medicaid: _____ n/a
Evenings: _____ n/a
Saturdays: _____ n/a
AmEx: _____ n/a
Visa/MC: _____ n/a

PATIENT COMMENTS

Very friendly and always attentive to my needs, especially when answering questions.

Really shows concern, adamant about yearly tests and screenings.

Shapiro, Irene, M.D.

GENERAL PRACTICE

	DOCTOR	OFFICE	OVERALL
	8.9	8.5	8.5

LANGUAGES	MEDICAL SCHOOL	HOSPITAL AFFILIATIONS
French Spanish	NYU '43	St Clares St Luke's-Roosevelt

Irene Shapiro, MD
65 Central Park West
246-8772

GENERAL OFFICE INFORMATION / **HMO/PPO**

First Visit: _____ $45
Regular Visit: ___ $45
Accessible: _____ Yes
Interpreters: ____ No
Medicare: _____ Yes
Medicaid: _____ No
Evenings: _____ No
Saturdays: _____ Yes
AmEx: _____ No
Visa/MC: _____ No

Blue Choice
Cigna
Independent Health

PATIENT COMMENTS

Does the job; nothing special.

Shay, William E., M.D.

INTERNAL MEDICINE

	DOCTOR	OFFICE	OVERALL
	8.5	7.6	9.2

LANGUAGES	MEDICAL SCHOOL	HOSPITAL AFFILIATIONS
Spanish	SUNY, Albany '81	St. Vincent's

William E Shay, MD
314 West 14 St
620-0144

GENERAL OFFICE INFORMATION		HMO/PPO
First Visit:	$150	Blue Choice
Regular Visit:	$90	Oxford
Accessible:	Yes	PHS/Guardian
Interpreters:	Yes	PHCS
Medicare:	Yes	United Healthcare
Medicaid:	No	
Evenings:	No	
Saturdays:	No	
AmEx:	No	
Visa/MC:	No	

PATIENT COMMENTS

Would suggest him highly.

He makes me very comfortable.

Shepard, Richard, D.O.

FAMILY PRACTICE

	DOCTOR	OFFICE	OVERALL
	7.5	7.3	7.8

LANGUAGES	MEDICAL SCHOOL	HOSPITAL AFFILIATIONS
Spanish	Osteo, Des Moines' 74	Beth Israel
		St Luke's-Roosevelt

Manhattan Medical Care
152 West 72 St
496-9620

GENERAL OFFICE INFORMATION		HMO/PPO
First Visit:	$85	Aetna/USH
Regular Visit:	n/a	Cigna
Accessible:	No	GHI
Interpreters:	No	NYC Care
Medicare:	Yes	Oxford
Medicaid:	No	Unified
Evenings:	No	United Healthcare
Saturdays:	Yes	
AmEx:	Yes	
Visa/MC:	Yes	

PATIENT COMMENTS

Some patients say:

good doctor; makes sure you understand everything and I really like him.

But others say:

take a magazine with you because you'll be waiting a long time, but you'll love him.

Sillay, Laila R., M.D.

OB/GYN

	DOCTOR	OFFICE	OVERALL
	9.3	9.1	9.6

LANGUAGES	MEDICAL SCHOOL	HOSPITAL AFFILIATIONS
Arabic	Univ. Texas '84	Lenox Hill
French		
Spanish		

Livoti, Sassoon, Sillay
MD, PC
266 East 78 St
288-1669

GENERAL OFFICE INFORMATION		HMO/PPO
First Visit:	$200	Private Practice
Regular Visit:	$170	
Accessible:	Yes	
Interpreters:	No	
Medicare:	No	
Medicaid:	No	
Evenings:	Yes	
Saturdays:	No	
AmEx:	Yes	
Visa/MC:	Yes	

PATIENT COMMENTS

Charming woman, a very nice lady and professional office and doctor.

Very caring, consistent and concerned.

Silverman, David, M.D.

INFECTIOUS DISEASES · INTERNAL MEDICINE

DOCTOR	OFFICE	OVERALL
8.5	8.4	9.0

LANGUAGES	MEDICAL SCHOOL	HOSPITAL AFFILIATIONS
Spanish	Columbia '76	NYU

David Silverman, MD
239 Central Park West
496-1929

GENERAL OFFICE INFORMATION	HMO/PPO
First Visit: _____ $225	Private Practice
Regular Visit: ___ $70	
Accessible: _____ Yes	
Interpreters: ____ Yes	
Medicare: _____ Yes	
Medicaid: _____ No	
Evenings: _____ Yes	
Saturdays: _____ No	
AmEx: _____ No	
Visa/MC: _____ Yes	

PATIENT COMMENTS

I love my doctor; funny guy and very good.

Skog, Donald R., M.D.

PEDIATRICS

DOCTOR	OFFICE	OVERALL
6.9	8.1	9.4

LANGUAGES	MEDICAL SCHOOL	HOSPITAL AFFILIATIONS
	UMDNJ '71	Lenox Hill
		NY Hospital-Cornell

Skog, Newman-Cedar &
Sacks
215 East 79 St
737-7800

GENERAL OFFICE INFORMATION	HMO/PPO
First Visit: _____ $125	Private Practice
Regular Visit: ___ $90	
Accessible: _____ No	
Interpreters: ____ No	
Medicare: _____ No	
Medicaid: _____ No	
Evenings: _____ Yes	
Saturdays: _____ No	
AmEx: _____ Yes	
Visa/MC: _____ Yes	

PATIENT COMMENTS

He's a good doctor and he always gets his job done well.

Smith, David I., M.D.

PEDIATRICS

DOCTOR	OFFICE	OVERALL
9.0	7.9	9.4

LANGUAGES	MEDICAL SCHOOL	HOSPITAL AFFILIATIONS
	NYU '56	NY Hospital-Cornell

David I. Smith, MD
450 East 69 St
988-0600

GENERAL OFFICE INFORMATION	HMO/PPO
First Visit: _____ $175	Private Practice
Regular Visit: ___ n/a	
Accessible: _____ Yes	
Interpreters: ____ No	
Medicare: _____ No	
Medicaid: _____ No	
Evenings: _____ No	
Saturdays: _____ No	
AmEx: _____ No	
Visa/MC: _____ Yes	

PATIENT COMMENTS

He's been my pediatrician for 18 years.

He's one of the family and great!

Snyder, Fredrick E., M.D.

DOCTOR	OFFICE	OVERALL
7.8	6.9	7.0

PEDIATRICS

LANGUAGES	MEDICAL SCHOOL	HOSPITAL AFFILIATIONS
	NY Med. '61	Lenox Hill

Fredric E. Snyder, MD
1009 Park Ave
879-3472

PATIENT COMMENTS

He's your average doctor.

GENERAL OFFICE INFORMATION	HMO/PPO
First Visit: _____ $95	
Regular Visit: ___ $95	
Accessible: _____ Yes	
Interpreters: ____ No	
Medicare: _____ No	
Medicaid: _____ No	
Evenings: _____ No	
Saturdays: _____ No	
AmEx: _____ No	
Visa/MC: _____ No	

Softness, Barney, M.D.

DOCTOR	OFFICE	OVERALL
8.1	7.7	8.4

PEDIATRIC ENOCRINOLOGY · PEDIATRICS

LANGUAGES	MEDICAL SCHOOL	HOSPITAL AFFILIATIONS
	Columbia '80	Columbia Presbyterian
		Lenox Hill
		NY Hospital-Cornell

West End Pediatrics
450 West End Ave
769-3070

PATIENT COMMENTS

Excellent and very good at returning emergency calls.

Very bad in keeping you waiting in crowded waiting room other sick kids.

GENERAL OFFICE INFORMATION	HMO/PPO
First Visit: _____ $125	Private Practice
Regular Visit: ___ $90	
Accessible: _____ Yes	
Interpreters: ____ No	
Medicare: _____ No	
Medicaid: _____ No	
Evenings: _____ Yes	
Saturdays: _____ No	
AmEx: _____ Yes	
Visa/MC: _____ Yes	

Solomon, David Y., M.D.

DOCTOR	OFFICE	OVERALL
8.2	7.7	7.7

INTERNAL MEDICINE · PHYSICAL MEDICINE

LANGUAGES	MEDICAL SCHOOL	HOSPITAL AFFILIATIONS
Arabic	Royal College,	Cabrini
French	Med, Iraq, '48	Gracie Sq
German		Lenox Hill
Persian		
Spanish		

David Y. Solomon, MD
440 East 79 St
535-4550

PATIENT COMMENTS

Hilarious, but could be a better doctor.

GENERAL OFFICE INFORMATION	HMO/PPO
First Visit: _____ $100	Aetna/USH
Regular Visit: ___ $70	Cigna
Accessible: _____ Yes	Magna Care
Interpreters: ____ No	NYC Care
Medicare: _____ Yes	United Healthcare
Medicaid: _____ Yes	
Evenings: _____ No	
Saturdays: _____ Yes	
AmEx: _____ No	
Visa/MC: _____ No	

Sorra, Lembitu, M.D.

INTERNAL MEDICINE

	DOCTOR	OFFICE	OVERALL
	9.5	8.9	9.4

LANGUAGES	MEDICAL SCHOOL	HOSPITAL AFFILIATIONS
	NY Med '77	Cabrini

Lembitu Sorra, MD
65 Central Park West
799-1990

GENERAL OFFICE INFORMATION	HMO/PPO
First Visit: _____ $300	Private Practice
Regular Visit: __ $130	
Accessible: _____ No	
Interpreters: ____ No	
Medicare: _____ Yes	
Medicaid: _____ No	
Evenings: _____ No	
Saturdays: _____ No	
AmEx: _____ Yes	
Visa/MC: _____ Yes	

PATIENT COMMENTS

Easy to talk to and a great listener. Cares about the whole person.

But, could be an excellent doctor if the staff were nicer.

Spielman, Gerald, M.D.

PEDIATRICS

	DOCTOR	OFFICE	OVERALL
	9.2	8.0	8.5

LANGUAGES	MEDICAL SCHOOL	HOSPITAL AFFILIATIONS
Spanish	Einstein'66	NY Hospital-Cornell

Gerald Spielman, MD
44 East 65 St
734-5655

GENERAL OFFICE INFORMATION	HMO/PPO
First Visit: _____ $150	Oxford
Regular Visit: __ $80	
Accessible: _____ No	
Interpreters: ____ No	
Medicare: _____ No	
Medicaid: _____ No	
Evenings: _____ No	
Saturdays: _____ No	
AmEx: _____ No	
Visa/MC: _____ No	

PATIENT COMMENTS

I like him and he's a good guy.

Very good, been with him since I was very young, my mother sees him as well.

Stein, Barry B., M.D.

PEDIATRICS

	DOCTOR	OFFICE	OVERALL
	9.0	8.9	9.4

LANGUAGES	MEDICAL SCHOOL	HOSPITAL AFFILIATIONS
Afrikkaans	Witwatersrand,	Lenox Hill
Hebrew	S. Africa, '80	Mount Sinai
Spanish		

Barry B. Stein, MD
1125 Park Ave.
289-1400

GENERAL OFFICE INFORMATION	HMO/PPO
First Visit: _____ n/a	Private Practice
Regular Visit: __ $100	
Accessible: _____ Yes	
Interpreters: ____ No	
Medicare: _____ No	
Medicaid: _____ No	
Evenings: _____ Yes	
Saturdays: _____ Yes	
AmEx: _____ No	
Visa/MC: _____ Yes	

PATIENT COMMENTS

Great with kids. Very kind.

Strauss, Steven, M.D.

DOCTOR	OFFICE	OVERALL
7.1	7.0	6.3

INTERNAL MEDICINE

LANGUAGES	MEDICAL SCHOOL	HOSPITAL AFFILIATIONS
Spanish	Geo. Wash. '78	Beth Israel
		Beth Israel North
		Mount Sinai

Steven Strauss MD
60 Gramercy Park North
477-9176

GENERAL OFFICE INFORMATION	HMO/PPO
First Visit: _____ $125	Aetna/USH
Regular Visit: ___ $85	Blue Choice
Accessible: _____ Yes	Cigna
Interpreters: ____ Yes	Magna Care
Medicare: _____ Yes	NYL Care
Medicaid: _____ No	Oxford
Evenings: _____ No	PHS/Guardian
Saturdays: _____ No	United Healthcare
AmEx: _____ No	
Visa/MC: _____ No	

PATIENT COMMENTS

Too many patients.

Doesn't give enough time to each patient and referrals and emergencies are a hassle.

Suozzi, William, M.D.

DOCTOR	OFFICE	OVERALL
8.5	7.7	8.1

INTERNAL MEDICINE

LANGUAGES	MEDICAL SCHOOL	HOSPITAL AFFILIATIONS
Spanish	Mt. Sinai, NY '84	Beth Israel
		Mount Sinai

Manhattan Primary Care
234 Central Park West
579-2200

GENERAL OFFICE INFORMATION	HMO/PPO
First Visit: _____ $225	Aetna/USH
Regular Visit: ___ $90	Chubb
Accessible: _____ Yes	Cigna
Interpreters: ____ No	Oxford
Medicare: _____ Yes	PHS/Guardian
Medicaid: _____ No	PHCS
Evenings: _____ Yes	United Healthcare
Saturdays: _____ No	
AmEx: _____ No	
Visa/MC: _____ Yes	

PATIENT COMMENTS

Some say:

Very good.

Answers own phone and personable, creates friendly environment.

But:

sometimes he doesn't seem to understand old people.

Sussman, Elihu, M.D.

DOCTOR	OFFICE	OVERALL
8.7	8.5	8.3

PEDIATRICS

LANGUAGES	MEDICAL SCHOOL	HOSPITAL AFFILIATIONS
	Boston '69	Beth Israel
		NYU
		St. Vincent's

Elihu Sussman, MD
24 East 12 St.
473-2900

GENERAL OFFICE INFORMATION	HMO/PPO
First Visit: _____ $80	Aetna/USH
Regular Visit: ___ $80	Healthsource
Accessible: _____ Yes	Oxford
Interpreters: ____ No	PHS/Guardian
Medicare: _____ No	United Healthcare
Medicaid: _____ No	
Evenings: _____ No	
Saturdays: _____ No	
AmEx: _____ No	
Visa/MC: _____ No	

PATIENT COMMENTS

Some say:

he's really good and friendly.

extremely efficient, never wait.

Other's say:

Very technical, not big in the personality department.

Tamarin, Steven, M.D.

FAMILY PRACTICE

	DOCTOR	OFFICE	OVERALL
	6.9	7.0	6.9

LANGUAGES	MEDICAL SCHOOL	HOSPITAL AFFILIATIONS
Spanish	Guadalajara, Mex '75	Beth Israel St Luke's-Roosevelt

Steven Tamarin, MD
441 West End Ave
496-2291

GENERAL OFFICE INFORMATION

First Visit: _____ $125
Regular Visit: ___ $90
Accessible: _____ No
Interpreters: ____ No
Medicare: _____ Yes
Medicaid: _____ No
Evenings: _____ Yes
Saturdays: _____ No
AmEx: _____ Yes
Visa/MC: _____ Yes

HMO/PPO

Aetna/USH
Atlantis
Bank Street
Chubb
Multiplan
Oxford
PHS/Guardian
PHCS

PATIENT COMMENTS

Some say:
does a good job.
Others feel:
he's overworked with too many patients.

Udesky, Robert A., M.D.

HEMATOLOGY · INTERNAL MEDICINE · MEDICAL ONCOLOGY

	DOCTOR	OFFICE	OVERALL
	8.2	8.4	8.1

LANGUAGES	MEDICAL SCHOOL	HOSPITAL AFFILIATIONS
	George Washington, St. Louis, '70	Beth Israel

Robert A. Udesky, MD
145 East 32 St.
725-5300

GENERAL OFFICE INFORMATION

First Visit: _____ n/a
Regular Visit: ___ n/a
Accessible: _____ n/a
Interpreters: ____ n/a
Medicare: _____ n/a
Medicaid: _____ n/a
Evenings: _____ n/a
Saturdays: _____ n/a
AmEx: _____ n/a
Visa/MC: _____ n/a

HMO/PPO

PATIENT COMMENTS

Ok for now, but I wish he was more forthcoming and personal.

Underberg, James A., M.D.

INTERNAL MEDICINE

	DOCTOR	OFFICE	OVERALL
	9.2	8.4	9.3

LANGUAGES	MEDICAL SCHOOL	HOSPITAL AFFILIATIONS
	Univ. of PA '86	Cabrini Joint Diseases NYU

Murray Hill Medical Group
317 East 34 St
726-7430

GENERAL OFFICE INFORMATION

First Visit: _____ n/a
Regular Visit: ___ n/a
Accessible: _____ Yes
Interpreters: ____ No
Medicare: _____ Yes
Medicaid: _____ No
Evenings: _____ Yes
Saturdays: _____ No
AmEx: _____ Yes
Visa/MC: _____ Yes

HMO/PPO

Aetna/USH
Healthsource
Oxford
Unified

PATIENT COMMENTS

Very good, pays a lot of attention to your particular concerns.

Probably the best doc I've ever had. All my friends no go to him. His referrals are as good as he is.

Very focused, well-mannered, intelligent.

Van Gilder, Max, M.D.

PEDIATRICS

DOCTOR	OFFICE	OVERALL
8.8	8.8	8.9

LANGUAGES	MEDICAL SCHOOL	HOSPITAL AFFILIATIONS
Spanish	Tulane '71	Columbia Presbyterian
		Lenox Hill
		St Luke's-Roosevelt

Westcare PC
241 Central Park West
787-1788

GENERAL OFFICE INFORMATION

PATIENT COMMENTS

GENERAL OFFICE INFORMATION	HMO/PPO
First Visit: _____ $175	Aetna/USH
Regular Visit: ___ $85	Blue Choice
Accessible: _____ No	Cigna
Interpreters: ____ No	NYC Care
Medicare: _____ No	Oxford
Medicaid: _____ No	PHS/Guardian
Evenings: _____ No	PHCS
Saturdays: _____ Yes	Pru Care
AmEx: _____ Yes	
Visa/MC: _____ Yes	

He is very good and very nice with the children.

Vizel-Schwartz, Monique, M.D.

HEMATOLOGY · INTERNAL MEDICINE · MEDICAL ONCOLOGY

DOCTOR	OFFICE	OVERALL
5.9	5.5	5.3

LANGUAGES	MEDICAL SCHOOL	HOSPITAL AFFILIATIONS
French	Brussels, Belg, '73	Beth Israel
Spanish		Cabrini
		NY Eye & Ear Infirmary
		St. Vincent's

Grenville Medical PC
70 East 10 St.
674-4455

PATIENT COMMENTS

GENERAL OFFICE INFORMATION	HMO/PPO
First Visit: _____ $150	Aetna/USH
Regular Visit: ___ $60	Cigna
Accessible: _____ Yes	HealthNet
Interpreters: ____ No	Magna Care
Medicare: _____ Yes	Oxford
Medicaid: _____ No	PHCS
Evenings: _____ Yes	Pru Care
Saturdays: _____ No	Unified
AmEx: _____ No	
Visa/MC: _____ No	

Her staff is rude and inefficient and she is not punctual. I will never go back again.

Wallach, Jeffrey, M.D.

INFECTIOUS DISEASES · INTERNAL MEDICINE

DOCTOR	OFFICE	OVERALL
9.2	9.2	9.2

LANGUAGES	MEDICAL SCHOOL	HOSPITAL AFFILIATIONS
	Guadalajara, Mex '80	Cabrini

Jeffrey Wallach, MD
24 East 12 St. #604
741-3030

PATIENT COMMENTS

GENERAL OFFICE INFORMATION	HMO/PPO
First Visit: _____ $325	Aetna/USH
Regular Visit: ___ $125	PHS/Guardian
Accessible: _____ Yes	
Interpreters: ____ No	
Medicare: _____ Yes	
Medicaid: _____ No	
Evenings: _____ Yes	
Saturdays: _____ No	
AmEx: _____ Yes	
Visa/MC: _____ Yes	

A good, attentive doctor. Recommended to all.

Weber, Scott, M.D.

DOCTOR	OFFICE	OVERALL
8.2	**8.2**	**8.3**

GASTROENTEROLOGY · INTERNAL MEDICINE

LANGUAGES	MEDICAL SCHOOL	HOSPITAL AFFILIATIONS
Spanish	NYU '88	NYU

Concorde Medical Group
232 East 30 St.
889-5544

GENERAL OFFICE INFORMATION	HMO/PPO
First Visit: _____ $150	Aetna/USH
Regular Visit: __ $110	Blue Choice
Accessible: _____ Yes	Chubb
Interpreters: ___ No	Oxford
Medicare: _____ Yes	PHCS
Medicaid: _____ No	United Healthcare
Evenings: _____ No	
Saturdays: _____ No	
AmEx: _____ Yes	
Visa/MC: _____ Yes	

PATIENT COMMENTS

Young and very attentive. But needs to be more personable and not rush.

Weiner, David J., M.D.

DOCTOR	OFFICE	OVERALL
9.2	**8.8**	**9.3**

INTERNAL MEDICINE

LANGUAGES	MEDICAL SCHOOL	HOSPITAL AFFILIATIONS
	NYU '73	Cabrini
		Lenox Hill
		St Luke's-Roosevelt

David J. Weiner, MD PC
206 East 30 St
686-6010

GENERAL OFFICE INFORMATION	HMO/PPO
First Visit: _____ $135	Blue Choice
Regular Visit: ___ $80	Chubb
Accessible: _____ Yes	Multiplan
Interpreters: ____ No	Oxford
Medicare: _____ Yes	Sanus
Medicaid: _____ No	Unified
Evenings: _____ No	
Saturdays: _____ No	
AmEx: _____ No	
Visa/MC: _____ No	

PATIENT COMMENTS

Best doc I've found since I've been an adult.

In touch with young people and issues, doesn't beat around the bush.

Gives practical advice, open-minded and very personal, has the ability to communicate on a human level.

Weinstein, Melvin, M.D.

DOCTOR	OFFICE	OVERALL
6.5	**7.1**	**7.0**

INTERNAL MEDICINE

LANGUAGES	MEDICAL SCHOOL	HOSPITAL AFFILIATIONS
Spanish	Einstein '71	Lenox Hill

Melvin Weinstein, MD
184 East 70 St
734-2756

GENERAL OFFICE INFORMATION	HMO/PPO
First Visit: _____ $175	Blue Choice
Regular Visit: ___ $85	Healthsource
Accessible: _____ Yes	Oxford
Interpreters: ____ No	PHS/Guardian
Medicare: _____ Yes	PHCS
Medicaid: _____ No	United Healthcare
Evenings: _____ No	
Saturdays: _____ No	
AmEx: _____ No	
Visa/MC: _____ No	

PATIENT COMMENTS

Some say:
he's very attentive and personable.
Others say:
it was a bad experience.

Weintraub, Gerald, M.D.

DOCTOR	OFFICE	OVERALL
8.6	9.1	8.0

GASTROENTEROLOGY · INTERNAL MEDICINE

LANGUAGES	MEDICAL SCHOOL	HOSPITAL AFFILIATIONS
Yiddish	NYU '54	St Luke's-Roosevelt

Gerald Weintrab, MD
74 East 90 St
348-4741

PATIENT COMMENTS

GENERAL OFFICE INFORMATION	HMO/PPO
First Visit: _____ $200	Chubb
Regular Visit: ___ $75	Oxford
Accessible: _____ No	PHS/Guardian
Interpreters: ____ No	PHCS
Medicare: _____ No	Pru Care
Medicaid: _____ No	
Evenings: _____ No	
Saturdays: _____ No	
AmEx: _____ No	
Visa/MC: _____ Yes	

Old style family practitioner. But I don't feel he addressed my concerns.

Weiser, Frank M., M.D.

DOCTOR	OFFICE	OVERALL
7.2	6.4	7.1

INTERNAL MEDICINE

LANGUAGES	MEDICAL SCHOOL	HOSPITAL AFFILIATIONS
German	Harvard '57	Beth Israel
Polish		Beth Israel North
Spanish		Mount Sinai
Tagalog		

Frank M Weiser, MD
715 Park Ave
288-5468

PATIENT COMMENTS

GENERAL OFFICE INFORMATION	HMO/PPO
First Visit: _____ n/a	Aetna/USH
Regular Visit: ___ n/a	Blue Choice
Accessible: _____ Yes	Chubb
Interpreters: ____ No	Cigna
Medicare: _____ Yes	Oxford
Medicaid: _____ No	PHS/Guardian
Evenings: _____ No	PHCS
Saturdays: _____ No	
AmEx: _____ No	
Visa/MC: _____ No	

Thorough at the beginning of my appointment, then loses it.

Not prepared ahead of time. When I get there he reads my chart and tries to remember who I am. It's like starting over each time.

Weiss, Nancy L., M.D.

DOCTOR	OFFICE	OVERALL
8.5	7.9	8.2

INTERNAL MEDICINE

LANGUAGES	MEDICAL SCHOOL	HOSPITAL AFFILIATIONS
	Einstein '85	Joint Diseases
		NYU

Concord Medical Group, PLLC
109 East 36 St
683-8105

PATIENT COMMENTS

GENERAL OFFICE INFORMATION	HMO/PPO
First Visit: _____ $170	Blue Choice
Regular Visit: __ $100	Healthsource
Accessible: _____ Yes	Independent Health
Interpreters: ____ No	Oxford
Medicare: _____ Yes	
Medicaid: _____ No	
Evenings: _____ No	
Saturdays: _____ Yes	
AmEx: _____ No	
Visa/MC: _____ Yes	

Young and friendly but tends to speak in medical jargon.

Weller, Alan S., M.D.

PEDIATRICS

DOCTOR	OFFICE	OVERALL
8.9	8.9	9.2

LANGUAGES	MEDICAL SCHOOL	HOSPITAL AFFILIATIONS
Spanish	Temple '92	NY Hospital-Cornell

Cornell Pediatric Faculty
Practice
428 East 72 St. #205
746-3325

GENERAL OFFICE INFORMATION | **HMO/PPO**

First Visit: _____ $150
Regular Visit: ___ $85
Accessible: _____ Yes
Interpreters: ____ No
Medicare: _____ No
Medicaid: _____ No
Evenings: _____ No
Saturdays: _____ Yes
AmEx: _____ Yes
Visa/MC: _____ Yes

Aetna/USH
Blue Choice
Cigna
Magna Care
Multiplan
Oxford
PHS/Guardian
PHCS
United Healthcare

PATIENT COMMENTS

He's an excellent physician.

My children refuse to be seen by anyone else if he's not available.

But others say:

A good doctor but too busy.

Wenger, Judith, M.D.

OB/GYN

DOCTOR	OFFICE	OVERALL
9.3	9.3	9.1

LANGUAGES	MEDICAL SCHOOL	HOSPITAL AFFILIATIONS
Hebrew	Northwestern '86	Lenox Hill
Spanish		NY Hospital-Cornell

Judith Wenger, MD
215 East 79 St.
628-9249

GENERAL OFFICE INFORMATION | **HMO/PPO**

First Visit: _____ $250
Regular Visit: __ $175
Accessible: _____ No
Interpreters: ____ No
Medicare: _____ No
Medicaid: _____ No
Evenings: _____ No
Saturdays: _____ No
AmEx: _____ No
Visa/MC: _____ No

Private Practice

PATIENT COMMENTS

Excellent, personable and clear.

Another says:

she's great, but spends so much time with each patient that she's always late.

Wiechowski, Michael, M.D.

GERIATRICS · INTERNAL MEDICINE

DOCTOR	OFFICE	OVERALL
7.8	7.9	8.7

LANGUAGES	MEDICAL SCHOOL	HOSPITAL AFFILIATIONS
Spanish	Guadalajara, Mex '81	St Luke's-Roosevelt

Central Park West Medical
2 West 86 St
769-4149

GENERAL OFFICE INFORMATION | **HMO/PPO**

First Visit: _____ $98
Regular Visit: ___ n/a
Accessible: _____ Yes
Interpreters: ____ No
Medicare: _____ Yes
Medicaid: _____ No
Evenings: _____ No
Saturdays: _____ Yes
AmEx: _____ Yes
Visa/MC: _____ Yes

Aetna/USH
Local 1199
United Healthcare

PATIENT COMMENTS

Humanistic in approach. He is careful not to over prescribe antibiotics.

Don't be afraid of his long hair.

But others say:

he sees too many patients at one time so you feel rushed.

Wishnick, Marcia M., M.D.

DOCTOR	OFFICE	OVERALL
9.2	9.1	9.4

PEDIATRICS

LANGUAGES	MEDICAL SCHOOL	HOSPITAL AFFILIATIONS
French	NYU '74	Beth Israel
Greek		Lenox Hill
Italian		Mount Sinai
Russian		NYU
Spanish		

Pediatrics East of NY, PC
157 East 81 St
879-7014

GENERAL OFFICE INFORMATION		HMO/PPO
First Visit: _____	n/a	Aetna/USH
Regular Visit: ___	n/a	Healthsource
Accessible: _____	Yes	Oxford
Interpreters: ____	No	Pru Care
Medicare: _____	No	
Medicaid: _____	No	
Evenings: _____	Yes	
Saturdays: _____	Yes	
AmEx: _____	No	
Visa/MC: _____	Yes	

PATIENT COMMENTS

Probably one of the best child care services in NYC.

Very personable, answers questions very well. Easy to understand.

Woronoff, Richard S., M.D.

DOCTOR	OFFICE	OVERALL
8.4	8.5	8.5

INTERNAL MEDICINE · PULMONOLOGY

LANGUAGES	MEDICAL SCHOOL	HOSPITAL AFFILIATIONS
	SUNY Downstate '66	St. Vincent's

Richard S. Woronoff, MD PC
36 Seventh Ave, Room 425
691-2622

GENERAL OFFICE INFORMATION		HMO/PPO
First Visit: _____	n/a	Aetna/USH
Regular Visit: ___	n/a	Blue Choice
Accessible: _____	Yes	Cigna
Interpreters: ____	No	Oxford
Medicare: _____	Yes	PHS/Guardian
Medicaid: _____	No	PHCS
Evenings: _____	No	Pru Care
Saturdays: _____	No	Sanus
AmEx: _____	No	
Visa/MC: _____	No	

PATIENT COMMENTS

Very business-like but in a good way.

Pleasant, good listener, cordial and good with follow-up

Yaffe, Bruce H., M.D.

DOCTOR	OFFICE	OVERALL
7.9	7.9	8.4

GASTROENTEROLOGY · INTERNAL MEDICINE

LANGUAGES	MEDICAL SCHOOL	HOSPITAL AFFILIATIONS
	G. Washington '76	Lenox Hill

Yaffe & Ruden Partnership
121 East 84 St
879-4700

GENERAL OFFICE INFORMATION		HMO/PPO
First Visit: _____	$90	Chubb
Regular Visit: ___	$90	Oxford
Accessible: _____	No	PHCS
Interpreters: ____	No	Unified
Medicare: _____	Yes	
Medicaid: _____	No	
Evenings: _____	Yes	
Saturdays: _____	No	
AmEx: _____	Yes	
Visa/MC: _____	Yes	

PATIENT COMMENTS

Great doctor but busy.

Others say:

He offers long waits for appointments, repeated busy signals and an uncomfortable lack of focus during consultations repeatedly interrupted by calls and you are put on "hold" forever.

Yale, Suzanne, M.D.

OB/GYN

DOCTOR	OFFICE	OVERALL
9.2	9.3	9.5

LANGUAGES	MEDICAL SCHOOL	HOSPITAL AFFILIATIONS
	UMDNJ '77	Lenox Hill

Dr. Romoff & Dr. Yale
768 Park Ave
744-9300

GENERAL OFFICE INFORMATION	HMO/PPO
First Visit: _____ $190	Private Practice
Regular Visit: __ $150	
Accessible: _____ Yes	
Interpreters: ____ Yes	
Medicare: _____ Yes	
Medicaid: _____ No	
Evenings: _____ No	
Saturdays: _____ No	
AmEx: _____ No	
Visa/MC: _____ No	

PATIENT COMMENTS

Efficient, professional, personable, dedicated and good.

Everyone in my office now sees her. I love her. I've been going to this doctor for 12 years.

She's both brilliant and gentle, a rare combination.

Yanoff, Allen, M.D.

INTERNAL MEDICINE

DOCTOR	OFFICE	OVERALL
7.6	7.8	7.9

LANGUAGES	MEDICAL SCHOOL	HOSPITAL AFFILIATIONS
	Einstein '66	Lenox Hill

Allen Yanoff, MD
9 East 63 St
593-7170

GENERAL OFFICE INFORMATION	HMO/PPO
First Visit: _____ n/a	Private Practice
Regular Visit: ___ n/a	
Accessible: _____ No	
Interpreters: ____ No	
Medicare: _____ No	
Medicaid: _____ No	
Evenings: _____ No	
Saturdays: _____ No	
AmEx: _____ Yes	
Visa/MC: _____ Yes	

PATIENT COMMENTS

He's outstanding, very personable and attentive.

I've recommended him to numerous friends. But very variable returning telephone calls.

Young, Kevin S., M.D.

INTERNAL MEDICINE

DOCTOR	OFFICE	OVERALL
9.5	9.1	9.6

LANGUAGES	MEDICAL SCHOOL	HOSPITAL AFFILIATIONS
Spanish	NYU '87	St Luke's-Roosevelt

Kevin S. Young, MD
415 West 57 St
582-6114

GENERAL OFFICE INFORMATION	HMO/PPO
First Visit: _____ $300	Healthsource
Regular Visit: __ $125	Oxford
Accessible: _____ No	
Interpreters: ____ No	
Medicare: _____ Yes	
Medicaid: _____ No	
Evenings: _____ No	
Saturdays: _____ No	
AmEx: _____ No	
Visa/MC: _____ Yes	

PATIENT COMMENTS

Very attentive and open-minded. Great office staff.

Knows how to make you feel good with whatever you have.

Zachary, Kirk J., M.D.

GASTROENTEROLOGY · INTERNAL MEDICINE

DOCTOR	OFFICE	OVERALL
8.0	8.3	8.2

LANGUAGES	MEDICAL SCHOOL	HOSPITAL AFFILIATIONS
	Columbia '77	Lenox Hill

Madison Medical Group
110 East 59 St.
583-2860

PATIENT COMMENTS

GENERAL OFFICE INFORMATION	HMO/PPO
First Visit: _____ $150	Aetna/USH
Regular Visit: ___ $85	Blue Choice
Accessible: _____ Yes	Chubb
Interpreters: _____ No	Magna Care
Medicare: _____ Yes	Oxford
Medicaid: _____ No	PHS/Guardian
Evenings: _____ No	PHCS
Saturdays: _____ No	
AmEx: _____ Yes	
Visa/MC: _____ Yes	

Pleasant, concerned and attentive.

Overall good doctor; I would recommend him.

Others say:

But could be a bit more personable.

Zilberstein, Inga, M.D.

OB/GYN

DOCTOR	OFFICE	OVERALL
9.0	9.1	9.6

LANGUAGES	MEDICAL SCHOOL	HOSPITAL AFFILIATIONS
Italian	NYU '86	Beth Israel North
Russian		Lenox Hill
Spanish		

Inga Zilberstein, MD
1317 Third Ave.
734-0187

PATIENT COMMENTS

GENERAL OFFICE INFORMATION	HMO/PPO
First Visit: _____ $175	Aetna/USH
Regular Visit: __ $125	Blue Choice
Accessible: _____ Yes	Cigna
Interpreters: _____ No	Healthsource
Medicare: _____ Yes	Oxford
Medicaid: _____ No	PHS/Guardian
Evenings: _____ Yes	Pru Care
Saturdays: _____ No	United Healthcare
AmEx: _____ No	
Visa/MC: _____ No	

I thought she was outstanding, efficient and had a grasp of my situation immediately.

She makes you feel very comfortable and is very concerned about her patient's welfare.

Accessibility Index

Adolescent Medicine
Pegler Cynthia, MD

Allergy & Immunology
Levine, Susan, MD
Lichtenfeld, Amy D., MD

Cardiology
Ellis, George C., MD
Franklin, Kenneth W., MD
Graf, Jeffrey H., MD
Kennish, Arthur, MD
Mattes, Leonard, MD
Mueller, Richard L., MD

Critical Care Medicine
Bahr, Gerald S., MD
Konecky, Alan, MD
Posner, David H., MD

Dermatology
Demar, Leon K., MD
Kling, Alan R., MD
Scheiner, Avery M., MD

Emergency Medicine
Lewin, Neal, A., MD

Endocrinology
Bernstein, Gerald, MD

Colt, Edward, MD
Park, Constance, MD

Family Practice
Aguero, Jose, MD
Buchel, Tamara L., MD
Chung, Bruce, MD
Clements, Jerry, MD
Goldberg, Richard, MD
Horowitz, Mark E., MD
Leeds, Gary, MD
Leichman, Gerald, MD
Olmscheid, Bruce, MD
Ravetz, Valerie, MD

Gastroenterology
Altman, Kenneth A., MD
Arons, Elliot, MD
Attia, Albert, MD
Baiocco, Peter, MD
Bearnot, Robert, MD
Brettholz, Edward, MD
Cantor, Michael C., MD
Goldberg, Edward S., MD
Loria, Jeffrey M., MD
Pearlman, Kenneth I., MD
Present, Daniel H., MD
Weber, Scott, MD
Zachary, Kirk J., MD

General Practice
Shapiro, Irene, MD

General Surgery
Cho, Sam K., MD

Geriatrics
Bernstein, Donald H., MD
Goodman, Karl, MD
Halper, Peter, MD
Mernick, Mitchel, MD
Schayes, Bernard, MD
Wiechowski, Michael, MD

Gynecology
Fishbane-Mayer, Jill, MD

Hematology
Buckner, Jeffrey A., MD
Edwards, Colleen A., MD
Frankel, Etta B., MD
Geltman, Richard L., MD
Lewin, Margaret, MD
Vizel-Schwartz, Monique, MD

Infectious Diseases
Bell, Evan T., MD
Fisher, Laura, MD
Fried, Richard P., MD
Gale, Robert K., MD
Hart, Catherine, MD
Levine, Susan, MD
Montana, John, MD
Nash, Thomas W., MD
Rudin, Debra, MD
Silverman, David, MD
Wallach, Jeffrey, MD

Internal Medicine
Abrams, Robert S., MD
Adler, Jack J., MD
Adler, Mitchell A., MD
Altman, Kenneth A., MD
Ament, Joseph D., MD

Amiraian, Richard H., MD
Arons, Elliot, MD
Attia, Albert, MD
Bahr, Gerald S., MD
Baiocco, Peter, MD
Bardes, Charles L., MD
Barnes, Edward, MD
Baskin, David H., MD
Bearnot, Robert, MD
Beitler, Martin, MD
Belenkov, Elliot, MD
Bell, Evan T., MD
Bendo, Dominick, MD
Bernstein, Donald H., MD
Bernstein, Gerald, MD
Blye, Ellen, MD
Brandon, Donald E., MD
Bregman, Zachary, MD
Brettholz, Edward, MD
Bruno, Peter J., MD
Buckner, Jeffrey A., MD
Burns, Margaret M., MD
Cantor, Michael C., MD
Charap, Peter, MD
Cohen, Albert, MD
Cohen, Robert L., MD
Colt, Edward, MD
De Cotis, Sue Gene, MD
Dhalla, Satish, MD
Diamond, Carol, MD
Edwards, Colleen A., MD
Ellis, George C., MD
Fallick, Nina, MD
Fisher, Laura, MD
Frankel, Etta B., MD
Franklin, Kenneth W., MD
Fried, Richard P., MD
Friedman, Jeffrey P., MD
Furman, Alice, MD
Gale, Robert K., MD
Geltman, Richard L., MD
Glick, Jeffrey, MD
Goldberg, Edward S., MD
Golden, Flavia A., MD

Goodman, Karl, MD
Graf, Jeffrey H., MD
Grossman, Howard A., MD
Halper, Peter, MD
Hammer, David, MD
Hart, Catherine, MD
Hauptman, Allen S., MD
Higgins, Lawrence A., DO, MPH
Horbar, Gary, MD
Kabakow, Bernard, MD
Kadet, Alan, MD
Kaufman, David L., MD
Keller, Raymond S., MD
Kennish, Arthur, MD
Klein, Susan, MD
Konecky, Alan, MD
Kramer, Sara, MD
Langelier, Carolyn A., MD
Leventhal, Gerald H., MD
Levine, Susan, MD
Lewin, Margaret, MD
Lewin, Neal A., MD
Lichtenfeld, Amy D., MD
Loria, Jeffrey M., MD
Lutsky, Eric, MD
Mattes, Leonard, MD
Mernick, Mitchel, MD
Montana, John, MD
Moyer, Lawson, MD
Mueller, Richard L., MD
Nash, Thomas W., MD
Nicolaides, Maria N., MD
Painter, Lucy N., MD
Palumbo, Michael J., MD
Park, Constance, MD
Pearlman, Kenneth I., MD
Perskin, Michael, MD
Pitaro, Gregory, MD
Posner, David H., MD
Present, Daniel H., MD
Rodman, John S., MD
Ruden, Ronald, MD
Rudin, Debra, MD
Schayes, Bernard, MD

Schwartz, Lawrence P., MD
Shay, William E., MD
Silverman, David, MD
Solomon, David Y., MD
Strauss, Steven, MD
Suozzi, William, MD
Underberg, James A., MD
Vizel-Schwartz, Monique, MD
Wallach, Jeffrey, MD
Weber, Scott, MD
Weiner, David J., MD
Weinstein, Melvin, MD
Weiser, Frank M., MD
Weiss, Nancy L., MD
Wiechowski, Michael, MD
Woronoff, Richard S., MD
Zachary, Kirk J., MD

Medical Oncology

Belenkov, Elliot, MD
Buckner, Jeffrey A., MD
Diamond, Carol, MD
Frankel, Etta B., MD
Geltman, Richard L., MD
Kabakow, Bernard, MD
Lewin, Margaret, MD
Mernick, Mitchel, MD
Vizel-Schwartz, Monique, MD

Nephrology

Nicolaides, Maria N., MD
Rodman, John S., MD

OB/GYN

Adler, Alan A., MD
Bello, Gaetano, MD
Berman, Alvin, MD
Brodman, Michael, MD
Carlon, Anne, MD
Corio, Laura, MD
Creatura, Chris, MD
Fischer, Ilene M., MD
Friedman, Lynn, MD
Goldman, Gary H., MD

OB/GYN (cont'd)

Gruss, Leslie, MD
Livoti, Carol, MD
Manos, Ellen, MD
Nachamie, Rebecca, MD
Park, Brian, MD
Sassoon, Albert K., MD, MPH
Sillay, Laila R., MD
Yale, Suzanne, MD
Zilberstein, Inga, MD

Pediatric Allergy

Lazarus, Herbert, MD

Pediatric Endocrinology

Rosenbaum, Michael, MD
Softness, Barney, MD

Pediatric Rheumatology

Lazarus, Herbert, MD

Pediatrics

Coffey, Robert J., MD
Daar, Eileen R., MD
Grunfeld, Paul, MD
Kahn, Max A., MD
Lantz, Howard, MD
Murphy, Ramon J. C., MD
Pasquariello, Palmo, MD
Pegler, Cynthia, MD

Rosenbaum, Michael, MD
Rosenfeld, Suzanne, MD
Schwartz, Stephen, MD
Smith, David I., MD
Snyder, Fredrick E., MD
Softness, Barney, MD
Stein, Barry B., MD
Sussman, Elihu, MD
Weller, Alan S., MD
Wishnick, Marcia M., MD

Physical Medicine & Rehabilitation

Solomon, David Y., MD

Pulmonolgy

Abrams, Robert S., MD
Adler, Jack J., MD
Bregman, Zachary, MD
Hammer, David, MD
Keller, Raymond S., MD
Konecky, Alan, MD
Nash, Thomas W., MD
Posner, David H., MD
Schwartz, Lawrence P., MD
Woronoff, Richard S., MD

Rheumatolgy

Bernstein, Donald H., MD
Kramer, Sara, MD

Hospital Affiliations

BEEKMAN HOSPITAL

See Downtown

BELLEVUE

1 Avenue A

Emergency Medicine

Lewin, Neal A., MD

Internal Medicine

Lewin, Neal A., MD

Pediatric Allergy

Lazarus, Herbert, MD

Pediatric Rheumatology

Lazarus, Herbert, MD

Pediatrics

Lazarus, Herbert, MD

BETH ISRAEL

First Avenue & 16 St.

Critical Care Medicine

Posner, David H., MD

Dermatology

Demar, Leon K., MD
Kling, Alan R., MD

Emergency Medicine

Isaacs, Daryl M., MD

Family Practice

Aguero, Jose, MD
Buchel, Tamara L., MD
Chung, Bruce, MD
Clements, Jerry, MD
Goldberg, Richard, MD
Horowitz, Mark E., MD
Leeds, Gary, MD
Leichman, Gerald, MD
Shepard, Richard, MD
Tamarin, Steven, MD

Gastroenterology

Brettholz, Edward, MD
Dubin, Richard, MD

Geriatrics

Halper, Peter, MD
Kamlet, David A., MD
Mernick, Mitchel, MD
Schayes, Bernard, MD

Hematology

Buckner, Jeffrey A., MD
Udesky, Robert A., MD
Vizel-Schwartz, Monique, MD

Internal Medicine

Beitler, Martin, MD

Internal Medicine (cont'd)

Bernstein, Stephen J., MD
Bregman, Zachary, MD
Brettholz, Edward, MD
Bruno, Peter J., MD
Buckner, Jeffrey A., MD
Charap, Peter, MD
De Cotis, Sue Gene, MD
Dubin, Richard, MD
Furman, Alice, MD
Glick, Jeffrey, MD
Halper, Peter, MD
Hammer, David, MD
Higgins, Lawrence A., DO, MPH
Isaacs, Daryl M., MD
Kabakow, Bernard, MD
Kamlet, David A., MD
Keller, Raymond S., MD
Leventhal, Gerald H., MD
Lutsky, Eric, MD
Mernick, Mitchel, MD
Nadel, Lester, MD
Posner, David H., MD
Schayes, Bernard, MD
Schwartz, Lawrence P., MD
Strauss, Steven, MD
Suozzi, William, MD
Udesky, Robert A., MD
Vizel-Schwartz, Monique, MD
Weiser, Frank M., MD

Medical Oncology

Buckner, Jeffrey A., MD
Kabakow, Bernard, MD
Mernick, Mitchel, MD
Udesky, Robert A., MD
Vizel-Schwartz, Monique, MD

OB/GYN

Fischer, Ilene M., MD
Gruss, Leslie, MD
Hobgood, Laura S., MD
Park, Brian, MD

Pediatric Pulmonology

Elbirt-Bender, Paula, MD

Pediatrics

Coffey, Robert J., MD
Elbirt-Bender, Paula, MD
Lantz, Howard, MD
Sussman, Elihu, MD
Wishnick, Marcia M., MD

Pulmonology

Bregman, Zachary, MD
Hammer, David, MD
Keller, Raymond S., MD
Posner, David H., MD
Schwartz, Lawrence P., MD

Rheumatolgy

Bernstein, Stephen J., MD
Leventhal, Gerald H., MD

BETH ISRAEL NORTH

170 East End Ave.

Allergy

Levine, Susan, MD
Lichtenfeld, Amy D., MD

Cardiovascular Diseases

Kennish, Arthur, MD

Critical Care Medicine

Bahr, Gerald S., MD

Family Practice

Levy, Albert, MD

Gastroenterology

Adler, Howard, MD
Goldberg, Edward S., MD
Loria, Jeffrey M., MD

General Surgery
Cho, Sam K., MD

Geriatrics
Levy, Albert, MD
Schayes, Bernard, MD

Hematology
Edwards, Colleen A., MD

Infectious Diseases
Levine, Susan, MD

Internal Medicine
Adler, Howard, MD
Adler, Jack J., MD
Ament, Joseph D., MD
Bahr, Gerald S., MD
Belenkov, Elliot, MD
Brandon, Donald E., MD
Edwards, Colleen A., MD
Fallick, Nina, MD
Goldberg, Edward S., MD
Hurd, Beverly, MD
Kennish, Arthur, MD
Klein, Susan, MD
Levine, Susan, MD
Lichtenfeld, Amy D., MD
Loria, Jeffrey M., MD
Radin, Allen, MD
Ruden, Ronald, MD
Schayes, Bernard, MD
Schwartz, Lawrence P., MD
Strauss, Steven, MD
Weiser, Frank M., MD

Medical Oncology
Belenkov, Elliot, MD

OB/GYN
Zilberstein, Inga, MD

Pediatrics
Kessler, Ruth E, MD

Pulmonary Medicine
Adler, Jack J., MD
Schwartz, Lawrence P., MD

Rheumatolgy
Radin, Allen, MD

CABRINI HOSPITAL
233 Third Ave

Endocrinology
Merker, Edward, MD

Family Practice
Goldberg, Richard, MD
Leeds, Gary, MD

Geriatrics
Kamlet, David A., MD
Mernick, Mitchel, MD
Schayes, Bernard, MD

Hematology
Vizel-Schwartz, Monique, MD

Infectious Diseases
Montana, John, MD
Wallach, Jeffrey, MD

Internal Medicine
Bernstein, Stephen J., MD
Bregman, Zachary, MD
Higgins, Lawrence A., DO, MPH
Kabakow, Bernard, MD
Kamlet, David A., MD
Lutsky, Eric, MD
Merker, Edward, MD
Mernick, Mitchel, MD
Montana, John, MD
Nadel, Lester, MD
Schayes, Bernard, MD
Solomon, David Y., MD
Sorra, Lembitu, MD

Internal Medicine (cont'd)

Underberg, James A., MD
Vizel-Schwartz, Monique, MD
Wallach, Jeffrey, MD
Weiner, David J, MD

Medical Oncology

Kabakow, Bernard, MD
Mernick, Mitchel, MD
Vizel-Schwartz, Monique, MD

Physical Medicine & Rehabilitation

Solomon, David Y., MD

Pulmonology

Bregman, Zachary, MD

Rheumatolgy

Bernstein, Stephen J., MD

COLUMBIA PRESBYTERIAN MEDICAL CENTER

3959 Broadway

Dermatology

Demar, Leon K., MD

Endocrinology

Park, Constance, MD

Infectious Diseases

Rudin, Debra, MD

Internal Medicine

Baskin, David H., MD
Nicolaides, Maria N., MD
Park, Constance, MD
Rudin, Debra, MD

Nephrology

Nicolaides, Maria N., MD

Pediatric Endocrinology

Softness, Barney, MD

Pediatrics

Softness, Barney, MD
Van Gilder, Max, MD

DOCTORS HOSPITAL

See Beth Israel North

DOWNTOWN HOSPITAL

170 William St

Emergency Medicine

Isaacs, Daryl M., MD

Gastroenterology

Bearnot, Robert, MD

Geriatrics

Goodman, Karl, MD

Infectious Diseases

Gale, Robert K., MD

Internal Medicine

Bearnot, Robert, MD
Bendo, Dominick, MD
Dhalla, Satish, MD
Gale, Robert K., MD
Goodman, Karl, MD
Isaacs, Daryl M., MD

GRACIE SQUARE HOSPITAL
420 East 76 St

Internal Medicine
Solomon, David Y., MD

Physical Medicine & Rehabilitation
Solomon, David Y., MD

HOSPITAL FOR JOINT DISEASES
301 East 17 St.

Geriatrics
Mernick, Mitchel, MD

Internal Medicine
Barnes, Edward, MD
Bernstein, Stephen J., MD
Friedman, Jeffrey P., MD
Kramer, Sara, MD
Leventhal, Gerald H., MD
Mernick, Mitchel, MD
Perskin, Michael, MD
Pitaro, Gregory, MD
Ruden, Ronald, MD
Schwartz, Lawrence P., MD
Underberg, James A., MD
Weiss, Nancy L., MD

Medical Oncology
Mernick, Mitchel, MD

Pulmonology
Schwartz, Lawrence P., MD

Rheumatolgy
Bernstein, Stephen J., MD
Kramer, Sara, MD
Leventhal, Gerald H., MD

LENOX HILL HOSPITAL
77 St & Park Ave.

Adolescent Medicine
Pegler, Cynthia, MD

Allergy
Lichtenfeld, Amy D., MD

Critical Care Medicine
Bahr, Gerald S., MD
Konecky, Alan, MD
Posner, David H., MD

Dermatology
Demar, Leon K., MD
Scheiner, Avery M., MD

Endocrinology
Bernstein, Gerald, MD
Merker, Edward, MD

Family Practice
Levy, Albert, MD

Gastroenterology
Baiocco, Peter, MD
Goldberg, Edward S., MD
Loria, Jeffrey M., MD
Yaffe, Bruce H., MD
Zachary, Kirk J., MD

Geriatrics
Levy, Albert, MD

Gynecology
Hirsch, Lissa, MD

Hematology
Lewin, Margaret, MD

Infectious Diseases
Bell, Evan T., MD

Internal Medicine

Abrams, Robert S., MD
Bahr, Gerald S., MD
Baiocco, Peter, MD
Belenkov, Elliot, MD
Bell, Evan T., MD
Bernstein, Gerald, MD
Bruno, Peter J., MD
Glick, Jeffrey, MD
Goldberg, Edward S., MD
Horbar, Gary, MD
Horovitz, H. Leonard, MD
Hurd, Beverly, MD
Konecky, Alan, MD
Lamm, Steven, MD
Leventhal, Gerald H., MD
Lewin, Margaret, MD
Lichtenfeld, Amy D., MD
Loria, Jeffrey M., MD
Merker, Edward, MD
Posner, David H., MD
Radin, Allen, MD
Rodman, John S., MD
Rooney, Ellen, MD
Ruden, Ronald, MD
Solomon, David Y., MD
Weiner, David J., MD
Weinstein, Melvin, MD
Yaffe, Bruce H., MD
Yanoff, Allen, MD
Zachary, Kirk J., MD

Medical Oncology

Belenkov, Elliot, MD
Lewin, Margaret, MD

Nephrology

Rodman, John S., MD

OB/GYN

Cavalli, Adele, MD
Chin Quee, Karlene, MD
Faroqui, Raufa, MD

Livoti, Carol, MD
Manos, Ellen, MD
Park, Brian, MD
Reiss, Ronald J., MD
Sassoon, Albert K., MD, MPH
Sillay, Laila R., MD
Wenger, Judith, MD
Yale, Suzanne, MD
Zilberstein, Inga, MD

Pediatric Allergy

Lazarus, Herbert, MD

Pediatric Endocrinology

Rosenbaum, Michael, MD
Softness, Barney, MD

Pediatric Pulmonology

Elbirt-Bender, Paula, MD

Pediatric Rheumatology

Lazarus, Herbert, MD

Pediatrics

Daar, Eileen R., MD
Elbirt-Bender, Paula, MD
Goldstein, Judith, MD
Grunfeld, Paul, MD
Kahn, Max A., MD
Kessler, Ruth E., MD
Khanna, Kussum, MD
Lantz, Howard, MD
Lazarus, Herbert, MD
Pasquariello, Palmo, MD
Pegler, Cynthia, MD
Rosenbaum, Michael, MD
Rosenfeld, Suzanne, MD
Seed, Wm, MD
Skog, Donald R., MD
Snyder, Fredrick E., MD
Softness, Barney, MD
Stein, Barry B., MD
Van Gilder, Max, MD
Wishnick, Marcia M., MD

Physical Medicine & Rehabilitation
Solomon, David Y., MD

Pulmonology
Abrams, Robert S., MD
Horovitz, H. Leonard, MD
Konecky, Alan, MD
Posner, David H., MD

Rheumatolgy
Leventhal, Gerald H., MD
Radin, Allen, MD

MANHATTAN EYE & EAR HOSPITAL
210 East 64 St.

Internal Medicine
Glick, Jeffrey, MD
Kabakow, Bernard, MD

Medical Oncology
Kabakow, Bernard, MD

MOUNT SINAI MEDICAL CENTER
Fifth Ave. & 101 St.

Cardiovascular Diseases
Graf, Jeffrey H., MD
Kennish, Arthur, MD
Mattes, Leonard, MD

Dermatology
Kling, Alan R., MD

Endocrinology
Merker, Edward, MD

Family Practice
Bauchman, Gail, MD

Gastroenterology
Present, Daniel H., MD

Gynecology
Berman, Joan K., MD
Fishbane-Mayer, Jill, MD

Hematology
Edwards, Colleen A., MD

Internal Medicine
Abrams, Robert S., MD
Adler, Jack J., MD
Charap, Peter, MD
Diamond, Carol, MD
Drapkin, Arnold, MD
Edwards, Colleen A., MD
Fallick, Nina, MD
Furman, Alice, MD
Graf, Jeffrey H., MD
Kennish, Arthur, MD
Mattes, Leonard, MD
Merker, Edward, MD
Present, Daniel H., MD
Strauss, Steven, MD
Suozzi, William, MD
Weiser, Frank M., MD

Medical Oncology
Diamond, Carol, MD

OB/GYN
Adler, Alan A., MD
Bello, Gaetano, MD
Berman, Alvin, MD
Brodman, Michael, MD
Corio, Laura, MD

OB/GYN (cont'd)

Friedman, Lynn, MD
Nachamie, Rebecca, MD

Pediatric Pulmonology

Elbirt-Bender, Paula, MD

Pediatrics

Elbirt-Bender, Paula, MD
Murphy, Ramon J. C., MD
Popper, Laura, MD
Stein, Barry B., MD
Wishnick, Marcia M., MD

Pulmonology

Abrams, Robert S., MD
Adler, Jack J., MD

NY EYE & EAR INFIRMARY

310 East 14 St.

Hematology

Vizel-Schwartz Monique, MD

Internal Medicine

Bernstein, Stephen J., MD
Horovitz, H. Leonard, MD
Vizel-Schwartz, Monique, MD

Medical Oncology

Vizel-Schwartz, Monique, MD

Pulmonology

Horovitz, H. Leonard, MD

Rheumatolgy

Bernstein, Stephen J., MD

NY HOSPITAL-CORNELL MEDICAL CENTER

521 East 68 St.

Adolescent Medicine

Pegler, Cynthia, MD

Allergy

Falk, George A., MD
Lichtenfeld, Amy D., MD

Cardiovascular Diseases

Andersen, Holly S., MD
Ellis, George C., MD
Franklin, Kenneth W., MD
Mueller, Richard L., MD

Gastroenterology

Cantor, Michael C., MD

Hematology

Geltman, Richard L., MD
Lewin, Margaret, MD

Infectious Diseases

Fisher, Laura, MD
Hart, Catherine, MD
Nash, Thomas W., MD

Internal Medicine

Andersen, Holly S., MD
Bardes, Charles L., MD
Belenkov, Elliot, MD
Cantor, Michael C., MD
Ellis, George C., MD
Falk, George A., MD
Fisher, Laura, MD
Franklin, Kenneth W., MD
Geltman, Richard L., MD
Golden, Flavia A., MD
Hart, Catherine, MD
Kadet, Alan, MD

Lewin, Margaret, MD
Lichtenfeld, Amy D., MD
Moyer, Lawson, MD
Mueller, Richard L., MD
Nash, Thomas W., MD
Painter, Lucy N., MD
Radin, Allen, MD
Rodman, John S., MD

Medical Oncology

Belenkov, Elliot, MD
Geltman, Richard L., MD
Lewin, Margaret, MD

Nephrology

Rodman, John S., MD

OB/GYN

Carlon, Anne, MD
Creatura, Chris, MD
Goldman, Gary H., MD
Lebowitz, Nancy, MD
Wenger, Judith, MD

Pediatric Endocrinology

Rosenbaum, Michael, MD
Softness, Barney, MD

Pediatrics

Goldstein, Judith, MD
Pegler, Cynthia, MD
Rosenbaum, Michael, MD
Rosenfeld, Suzanne, MD
Seed, Wm, MD
Skog, Donald R., MD
Smith, David I., MD
Softness, Barney, MD
Spielman, Gerald, MD
Weller, Alan S., MD

Pulmonology

Falk, George A., MD
Nash, Thomas W., MD

Rheumatolgy

Radin, Allen, MD

NYU MEDICAL CENTER

550 First Ave.

Dermatology

Scheiner, Avery M., MD

Emergency Medicine

Lewin, Neal A., MD

Gastroenterology

Bearnot, Robert, MD
Lustbader, Ian, MD
Pearlman, Kenneth I., MD
Weber, Scott, MD

Gynecology

Hirsch, Lissa, MD

Hematology

Buckner, Jeffrey A., MD

Infectious Diseases

Silverman, David, MD

Internal Medicine

Adler, Mitchell A., MD
Barnes, Edward, MD
Bearnot, Robert, MD
Brandon, Donald E., MD
Buckner, Jeffrey A., MD
Friedman, Jeffrey P., MD
Hauptman, Allen S., MD
Kennedy, James T., MD
Kramer, Sara, MD
Lamm, Steven, MD

Internal Medicine (cont'd)

Langelier, Carolyn A., MD
Lewin, Neal A., MD
Lustbader, Ian, MD
Newman, Mark R., MD
Palumbo, Michael J., MD
Pearlman, Kenneth I., MD
Perskin, Michael, MD
Pitaro, Gregory, MD
Silverman, David, MD
Underberg, James A., MD
Weber, Scott, MD
Weiss, Nancy L., MD

Medical Oncology

Buckner, Jeffrey A., MD

OB/GYN

Ho, Alison, MD
Selick, Caryn E., MD

Pediatric Allergy

Lazarus, Herbert, MD

Pediatric Rheumatology

Lazarus, Herbert, MD

Pediatrics

Kahn, Max A., MD
Lazarus, Herbert, MD
Schwartz, Stephen, MD
Sussman, Elihu, MD
Wishnick, Marcia M., MD

Rheumatolgy

Kramer, Sara, MD

HOSPITAL FOR SPECIAL SURGERY
535 East 70 St.

Cardiovascular Diseases

Franklin, Kenneth W., MD

Internal Medicine

Franklin, Kenneth W., MD

ST CLARE'S HOSPITAL
415 West 51 St.

General Practice

Shapiro, Irene, MD

ST LUKE'S-ROOSEVELT HOSPITAL
1000 Tenth Ave.

Cardiovascular Diseases

Mueller, Richard L., MD

Dermatology

Demar, Leon K., MD

Endocrinology

Colt, Edward, MD

Family Practice

Aguero, Jose, MD
Bauchman, Gail, MD
Levy, Albert, MD
Shepard, Richard, MD
Tamarin, Steven, MD

Gastroenterology

Altman, Kenneth A., MD
Arons, Elliot, MD
Attia, Albert, MD
Weintraub, Gerald, MD

General Practice

Shapiro, Irene, MD

Geriatrics

Babitz, Lisa E., MD
Goodman, Karl, MD
Kamlet, David A., MD
Levy, Albert, MD
Wiechowski, Michael, MD

Gynecology

Beitner, Orit, MD

Hematology

Beautyman, Elizabeth J., MD
Frankel, Etta B., MD
Lewin, Margaret, MD

Infectious Diseases

Fried, Richard P., MD

Internal Medicine

Altman, Kenneth A., MD
Amiraian, Richard H., MD
Arons, Elliot, MD
Attia, Albert, MD
Babitz, Lisa E., MD
Baskin, David H., MD
Beautyman, Elizabeth J., MD
Bendo, Dominick, MD
Blye, Ellen, MD
Cohen, Albert, MD
Colt, Edward, MD
Frankel, Etta B., MD
Fried, Richard P., MD
Goodman, Karl, MD
Grossman, Howard A., MD
Hurd, Beverly, MD
Kadet, Alan, MD
Kamlet, David A., MD
Larson, Carol, MD
Lewin, Margaret, MD
Mueller, Richard L., MD

Weiner, David J., MD
Weintraub, Gerald, MD
Wiechowski, Michael, MD
Young, Kevin S., MD

Medical Oncology

Frankel, Etta B., MD
Lewin, Margaret, MD

OB/GYN

Faroqui, Raufa, MD
Manos, Ellen, MD
Selick, Caryn E., MD

Pediatric Allergy

Lazarus, Herbert, MD

Pediatric Rheumatology

Lazarus, Herbert, MD

Pediatrics

Kahn, Max A., MD
Khanna, Kussum, MD
Lazarus, Herbert, MD
Van Gilder, Max, MD

ST. VINCENT'S HOSPITAL

241 West 30 St.

Endocrinology

Colt, Edward, MD

Family Practice

Braun, James F., MD
Clements, Jerry, MD
Olmscheid, Bruce, MD
Ravetz, Valerie, MD

Geriatrics

Bernstein, Donald H., MD

Hematology

Vizel-Schwartz, Monique, MD

Internal Medicine

Amiraian, Richard H., MD
Bernstein, Donald H., MD
Burns, Margaret M., MD
Cohen, Robert L., MD
Colt, Edward, MD
Dhalla, Satish, MD
Higgins, Lawrence A., DO, MPH
Kaufman, David L., MD
Mellow, Nancy L., MD
Nadel, Lester, MD
Shay, William E., MD
Vizel-Schwartz, Monique, MD
Woronoff, Richard S., MD

Medical Oncology

Vizel-Schwartz, Monique, MD

OB/GYN

Cavalli, Adele, MD

Pediatrics

Coffey, Robert J., MD
Sussman, Elihu, MD

Pulmonary Medicine

Woronoff, Richard S., MD

Rheumatolgy

Bernstein, Donald H., MD

Insurance Providers

AETNA/USH

Allergy & Immunology
Levine, Susan, MD
Lichtenfeld, Amy D., MD

Cardiology
Graf, Jeffrey H., MD
Kennish, Arthur, MD
Mattes, Leonard, MD
Mueller, Richard L., MD

Critical Care Medicine
Posner, David H., MD

Dermatology
Kling, Alan R., MD
Scheiner, Avery M., MD

Endocrinology
Colt, Edward, MD
Merker, Edward, MD

Family Practice
Aguero, Jose, MD
Braun, James F., MD
Buchel, Tamara L., MD
Chung, Bruce, MD
Goldberg, Richard, MD
Horowitz, Mark E., MD
Leeds, Gary, MD
Leichman, Gerald, MD
Levy, Albert, MD

Olmscheid, Bruce, MD
Ravetz, Valerie, MD
Shepard, Richard, MD
Tamarin, Steven, MD

Gastroenterology
Arons, Elliot, MD
Baiocco, Peter, MD
Brettholz, Edward, MD
Goldberg, Edward S., MD
Loria, Jeffrey M., MD
Pearlman, Kenneth I., MD
Weber, Scott, MD
Zachary, Kirk J., MD

Geriatrics
Babitz, Lisa E., MD
Bernstein, Donald H., MD
Goodman, Karl, MD
Halper, Peter, MD
Levy, Albert, MD
Mernick, Mitchel, MD
Schayes, Bernard, MD
Wiechowski, Michael, MD

Hematology
Edwards, Colleen A., MD
Frankel, Etta B., MD
Vizel-Schwartz, Monique, MD

Infectious Diseases
Fried, Richard P., MD
Levine, Susan, MD

Infectious Diseases (cont'd)

Montana, John, MD
Wallach, Jeffrey, MD

Internal Medicine

Ament, Joseph D., MD
Amiraian, Richard H., MD
Arons, Elliot, MD
Babitz, Lisa E., MD
Baiocco, Peter, MD
Bardes, Charles L., MD
Barnes, Edward, MD
Baskin, David H., MD
Bernstein, Donald H., MD
Bernstein, Stephen J., MD
Blye, Ellen, MD
Bregman, Zachary, MD
Brettholz, Edward, MD
Bruno, Peter J., MD
Charap, Peter, MD
Colt, Edward, MD
Dhalla, Satish, MD
Edwards, Colleen A., MD
Fallick, Nina, MD
Frankel, Etta B., MD
Fried, Richard P., MD
Furman, Alice, MD
Glick, Jeffrey, MD
Goldberg, Edward S., MD
Golden, Flavia A., MD
Goodman, Karl, MD
Graf, Jeffrey H., MD
Grossman, Howard A., MD
Halper, Peter, MD
Hammer, David, MD
Hauptman, Allen S., MD
Hurd, Beverly, MD
Kadet, Alan, MD
Kaufman, David L., MD
Keller, Raymond S., MD
Kennish, Arthur, MD
Klein, Susan, MD

Kramer, Sara, MD
Leventhal, Gerald H., MD
Levine, Susan, MD
Lichtenfeld, Amy D., MD
Loria, Jeffrey M., MD
Lutsky, Eric, MD
Mattes, Leonard, MD
Merker, Edward, MD
Mernick, Mitchel, MD
Montana, John, MD
Moyer, Lawson, MD
Mueller, Richard L., MD
Nadel, Lester, MD
Nicolaides, Maria N., MD
Painter, Lucy N., MD
Palumbo, Michael J., MD
Pearlman, Kenneth I., MD
Perskin, Michael, MD
Pitaro, Gregory, MD
Posner, David H., MD
Radin, Allen, MD
Ruden, Ronald, MD
Schayes, Bernard, MD
Schwartz, Lawrence P., MD
Solomon, David Y., MD
Strauss, Steven, MD
Suozzi, William, MD
Underberg, James A., MD
Vizel-Schwartz, Monique, MD
Wallach, Jeffrey, MD
Weber, Scott, MD
Weiser, Frank M., MD
Wiechowski, Michael, MD
Woronoff, Richard S., MD
Zachary, Kirk J., MD

Medical Oncology

Frankel, Etta B., MD
Mernick, Mitchel, MD
Vizel-Schwartz, Monique, MD

Nephrology

Nicolaides, Maria N., MD

OB/GYN

Adler, Alan A., MD
Brodman, Michael, MD
Fischer, Ilene M., MD
Hobgood, Laura S., MD
Reiss, Ronald J., MD
Zilberstein, Inga, MD

Pediatrics

Coffey, Robert J., MD
Daar, Eileen R., MD
Grunfeld, Paul, MD
Kessler, Ruth E., MD
Khanna, Kussum, MD
Sussman, Elihu, MD
Van Gilder, Max, MD
Weller, Alan S., MD
Wishnick, Marcia M., MD

Physical Medicine & Rehabilitation

Solomon, David Y., MD

Pulmonology

Bregman, Zachary, MD
Hammer, David, MD
Keller, Raymond S., MD
Posner, David H., MD
Schwartz, Lawrence P., MD
Woronoff, Richard S., MD

Rheumatolgy

Bernstein, Donald H., MD
Bernstein, Stephen J., MD
Kramer, Sara, MD
Leventhal, Gerald H., MD
Radin, Allen, MD

AFFORDABLE NETWORK

Dermatology

Kling, Alan R., MD

Internal Medicine

Lamm, Steven, MD

AHP

Internal Medicine

Bruno, Peter J., MD

ANTHEM HEALTH

Geriatrics

Mernick, Mitchel, MD

Internal Medicine

Diamond, Carol, MD
Lutsky, Eric, MD
Mernick, Mitchel, MD
Moyer, Lawson, MD

Medical Oncology

Diamond, Carol, MD
Mernick, Mitchel, MD

ATLANTIS

Family Practice

Tamarin, Steven, MD

BANK STREET

Family Practice

Braun, James F., MD
Tamarin, Steven, MD

BLUE CHOICE

Allergy & Immunology
Lichtenfeld, Amy D., MD

Cardiology
Graf, Jeffrey H., MD
Kennish, Arthur, MD
Mattes, Leonard, MD
Mueller, Richard L., MD

Critical Care Medicine
Konecky, Alan, MD
Posner, David H., MD

Emergency Medicine
Isaacs, Daryl M., MD

Endocrinology
Colt, Edward, MD
Merker, Edward, MD

Family Practice
Chung, Bruce, MD
Goldberg, Richard, MD
Horowitz, Mark E., MD
Leeds, Gary, MD
Olmscheid, Bruce, MD
Ravetz, Valerie, MD

Gastroenterology
Adler, Howard, MD
Arons, Elliot, MD
Baiocco, Peter, MD
Brettholz, Edward, MD
Goldberg, Edward S., MD
Lustbader, Ian, MD
Weber, Scott, MD
Zachary, Kirk J., MD

General Practice
Shapiro, Irene, MD

General Surgery
Cho, Sam K., MD

Geriatrics
Babitz, Lisa E., MD
Bernstein, Donald H., MD
Kamlet, David A., MD
Mernick, Mitchel, MD
Schayes, Bernard, MD

Hematology
Buckner, Jeffrey A., MD
Edwards, Colleen A., MD
Frankel, Etta B., MD
Geltman, Richard L., MD

Infectious Diseases
Montana, John, MD

Internal Medicine
Abrams, Robert S., MD
Adler, Howard, MD
Adler, Jack J., MD
Ament, Joseph D., MD
Amiraian, Richard H., MD
Arons, Elliot, MD
Babitz, Lisa E., MD
Baiocco, Peter, MD
Bardes, Charles L., MD
Belenkov, Elliot, MD
Bendo, Dominick, MD
Bernstein, Donald H., MD
Brandon, Donald E., MD
Bregman, Zachary, MD
Brettholz, Edward, MD
Bruno, Peter J., MD
Buckner, Jeffrey A., MD
Burns, Margaret M., MD
Cohen, Albert, MD
Cohen, Robert L., MD
Colt, Edward, MD

Diamond, Carol, MD
Edwards, Colleen A., MD
Fallick, Nina, MD
Frankel, Etta B., MD
Geltman, Richard L., MD
Glick, Jeffrey, MD
Goldberg, Edward S., MD
Graf, Jeffrey H., MD
Hurd, Beverly, MD
Isaacs, Daryl M., MD
Kabakow, Bernard, MD
Kadet, Alan, MD
Kamlet, David A., MD
Keller, Raymond S., MD
Kennish, Arthur, MD
Klein, Susan, MD
Konecky, Alan, MD
Kramer, Sara, MD
Lichtenfeld, Amy D., MD
Lustbader, Ian, MD
Lutsky, Eric, MD
Mattes, Leonard, MD
Merker, Edward, MD
Mernick, Mitchel, MD
Montana, John, MD
Moyer, Lawson, MD
Mueller, Richard L., MD
Nicolaides, Maria N., MD
Painter, Lucy N., MD
Posner, David H., MD
Radin, Allen, MD
Ruden, Ronald, MD
Schayes, Bernard, MD
Schwartz, Lawrence P., MD
Shay, William E., MD
Strauss, Steven, MD
Weber, Scott, MD
Weiner, David J., MD
Weinstein, Melvin, MD
Weiser, Frank M., MD
Weiss, Nancy L., MD
Woronoff, Richard S., MD
Zachary, Kirk J., MD

Medical Oncology

Belenkov, Elliot, MD
Buckner, Jeffrey A., MD
Diamond, Carol, MD
Frankel, Etta B., MD
Geltman, Richard L., MD
Kabakow, Bernard, MD
Mernick, Mitchel, MD

Nephrology

Nicolaides, Maria N., MD

OB/GYN

Fischer, Ilene M., MD
Hobgood, Laura S., MD
Reiss, Ronald J., MD
Zilberstein., Inga, MD

Pediatrics

Coffey, Robert J., MD
Goldstein, Judith, MD
Grunfeld, Paul, MD
Kessler, Ruth E., MD
Van Gilder, Max, MD
Weller, Alan S., MD

Pulmonology

Abrams, Robert S., MD
Adler, Jack J., MD
Bregman, Zachary, MD
Keller, Raymond S., MD
Konecky, Alan, MD
Posner, David H., MD
Schwartz, Lawrence P., MD
Woronoff, Richard S., MD

Rheumatolgy

Bernstein, Donald H., MD
Kramer, Sara, MD
Radin, Allen, MD

CAMBRIDGE

Gastroenterology
Attia, Albert, MD

Internal Medicine
Attia, Albert, MD

CHUBB

Cardiology
Graf, Jeffrey H., MD
Kennish, Arthur, MD

Critical Care Medicine
Konecky, Alan, MD

Dermatology
Demar, Leon K., MD
Kling, Alan R., MD

Emergency Medicine
Isaacs, Daryl M., MD
Lewin, Neal A., MD

Family Practice
Aguero, Jose, MD
Braun, James F., MD
Levy, Albert, MD
Tamarin, Steven, MD

Gastroenterology
Arons, Elliot, MD
Attia, Albert, MD
Loria, Jeffrey M., MD
Weber, Scott, MD
Weintraub, Gerald, MD
Yaffe, Bruce H., MD
Zachary, Kirk J., MD

Geriatrics
Babitz, Lisa E., MD
Levy, Albert, MD

Hematology
Beautyman, Elizabeth J., MD

Infectious Diseases
Fried, Richard P., MD

Internal Medicine
Abrams, Robert S., MD
Adler, Mitchell A., MD
Arons, Elliot, MD
Attia, Albert, MD
Babitz, Lisa E., MD
Beautyman, Elizabeth J., MD
Bruno, Peter J., MD
Charap, Peter, MD
Cohen, Albert, MD
Diamond, Carol, MD
Fallick, Nina, MD
Fried, Richard P., MD
Friedman, Jeffrey P., MD
Graf, Jeffrey H., MD
Hauptman, Allen S., MD
Isaacs, Daryl M., MD
Kabakow, Bernard, MD
Kaufman, David L., MD
Kennish, Arthur, MD
Konecky, Alan, MD
Lamm, Steven, MD
Lewin, Neal A., MD
Loria, Jeffrey M., MD
Pitaro, Gregory, MD
Ruden, Ronald, MD
Suozzi, William, MD
Weber, Scott, MD
Weiner, David J., MD
Weintraub, Gerald, MD
Weiser, Frank M., MD
Yaffe, Bruce H., MD
Zachary, Kirk J., MD

Medical Oncology
Diamond, Carol, MD
Kabakow, Bernard, MD

OB/GYN

Corio, Laura, MD
Fischer, Ilene M., MD
Ho, Alison, MD
Reiss, Ronald J., MD

Pediatrics

Goldstein, Judith, MD
Grunfeld, Paul, MD
Pasquariello, Palmo, MD

Pulmonology

Abrams, Robert S., MD
Konecky, Alan, MD

CIGNA

Allergy & Immunology

Lichtenfeld, Amy D., MD

Cardiology

Graf, Jeffrey H., MD
Mueller, Richard L., MD

Critical Care Medicine

Bahr, Gerald S., MD
Konecky, Alan, MD

Family Practice

Aguero, Jose, MD
Buchel, Tamara L., MD
Chung, Bruce, MD
Goldberg, Richard, MD
Leeds, Gary, MD
Levy, Albert, MD
Shepard, Richard, MD

Gastroenterology

Arons, Elliot, MD
Attia, Albert, MD
Baiocco, Peter, MD
Loria, Jeffrey M., MD

General Practice

Shapiro, Irene, MD

Geriatrics

Levy, Albert, MD
Mernick, Mitchel, MD
Schayes, Bernard, MD

Hematology

Edwards, Colleen A., MD
Frankel, Etta B., MD
Lewin, Margaret, MD
Vizel-Schwartz, Monique, MD

Infectious Diseases

Bell, Evan T., MD
Fisher, Laura, MD
Fried, Richard P., MD

Internal Medicine

Arons, Elliot, MD
Attia, Albert, MD
Bahr, Gerald S., MD
Baiocco, Peter, MD
Belenkov, Elliot, MD
Bell, Evan T., MD
Bendo, Dominick, MD
Bernstein, Stephen J., MD
Brandon, Donald E., MD
Bregman, Zachary, MD
Charap, Peter, MD
Cohen, Albert, MD
Dhalla, Satish, MD
Edwards, Colleen A., MD
Fallick, Nina, MD
Fisher, Laura, MD
Frankel, Etta B., MD
Fried, Richard P., MD
Glick, Jeffrey, MD
Graf, Jeffrey H., MD
Grossman, Howard A., MD
Hurd, Beverly, MD
Kabakow, Bernard, MD

Internal medicine (cont'd)

Kadet, Alan, MD
Keller, Raymond S., MD
Klein, Susan, MD
Konecky, Alan, MD
Kramer, Sara, MD
Lewin, Margaret, MD
Lichtenfeld, Amy D., MD
Loria, Jeffrey M., MD
Lutsky, Eric, MD
Mernick, Mitchel, MD
Mueller, Richard L., MD
Nadel, Lester, MD
Radin, Allen, MD
Schayes, Bernard, MD
Solomon, David Y., MD
Strauss, Steven, MD
Suozzi, William, MD
Vizel-Schwartz, Monique, MD
Weiser, Frank M., MD
Woronoff, Richard S., MD

Medical Oncology

Belenkov, Elliot, MD
Frankel, Etta B., MD
Kabakow, Bernard, MD
Lewin, Margaret, MD
Mernick, Mitchel, MD
Vizel-Schwartz, Monique, MD

OB/GYN

Adler, Alan A., MD
Fischer, Ilene M., MD
Park, Brian, MD
Zilberstein, Inga, MD

Pediatrics

Goldstein, Judith, MD
Kessler, Ruth E., MD
Khanna, Kussum, MD
Van Gilder, Max, MD
Weller, Alan S., MD

Physical Medicine & Rehab.

Solomon, David Y., MD

Pulmonology

Bregman, Zachary, MD
Keller, Raymond S., MD
Konecky, Alan, MD
Woronoff, Richard S., MD

Rheumatolgy

Bernstein, Stephen J., MD
Kramer, Sara, MD
Radin, Allen, MD

EMPIRE

Family Practice

Aguero, Jose, MD

Gastroenterology

Attia, Albert, MD

Internal Medicine

Attia, Albert, MD

GHI

Family Practice

Shepard, Richard, MD

Gastroenterology

Lustbader, Ian, MD

Internal Medicine

Glick, Jeffrey, MD
Lustbader, Ian, MD

HEALTH EASE

Cardiology
Mattes, Leonard, MD

Critical Care Medicine
Konecky, Alan, MD

Endocrinology
Colt, Edward, MD

Hematology
Edwards, Colleen A., MD

Internal Medicine
Amiraian, Richard H., MD
Belenkov, Elliot, MD
Colt, Edward, MD
Edwards, Colleen A., MD
Konecky, Alan, MD
Mattes, Leonard, MD

Medical Oncology
Belenkov, Elliot, MD

Pediatrics
Kessler, Ruth E., MD

Pulmonology
Konecky, Alan, MD

HEALTHNET

Cardiology
Graf, Jeffrey H., MD
Mattes, Leonard, MD

Geriatrics
Kamlet, David A., MD

Hematology
Vizel-Schwartz, Monique, MD

Internal Medicine
Amiraian, Richard H., MD
Belenkov, Elliot, MD
Bendo, Dominick, MD
Graf, Jeffrey H., MD
Kabakow, Bernard, MD
Kamlet, David A., MD
Mattes, Leonard, MD
Vizel-Schwartz, Monique, MD

Medical Oncology
Belenkov, Elliot, MD
Kabakow, Bernard, MD
Vizel-Schwartz, Monique, MD

HEALTHSOURCE

Endocrinology
Park, Constance, MD

Gastroenterology
Baiocco, Peter, MD
Lustbader, Ian, MD
Pearlman, Kenneth I., MD

Internal Medicine
Baiocco, Peter, MD
Barnes, Edward, MD
Baskin, David H., MD
Bernstein, Stephen J., MD
Blye, Ellen, MD
Glick, Jeffrey, MD
Grossman, Howard A., MD
Horbar, Gary, MD
Hurd, Beverly, MD
Kennedy, James T., MD
Kramer, Sara, MD
Lustbader, Ian, MD
Painter, Lucy N., MD
Palumbo, Michael J., MD
Park, Constance, MD
Pearlman, Kenneth I., MD

Internal medicine (cont'd)

Perskin, Michael, MD
Radin, Allen, MD
Underberg, James A., MD
Weinstein, Melvin, MD
Weiss, Nancy L., MD
Young, Kevin S., MD

OB/GYN

Zilberstein, Inga, MD

Pediatrics

Sussman, Elihu, MD
Wishnick, Marcia M., MD

Rheumatolgy

Bernstein, Stephen J., MD
Kramer, Sara, MD
Radin, Allen, MD

INDEPENDENT HEALTH

Gastroenterology

Goldberg, Edward S., MD

General Practice

Shapiro, Irene, MD

General Surgery

Cho, Sam K., MD

Geriatrics

Mernick, Mitchel, MD

Internal Medicine

Goldberg, Edward S., MD
Mernick, Mitchel, MD
Weiss, Nancy L., MD

Medical Oncology

Mernick, Mitchel, MD

Pediatrics

Kessler, Ruth E., MD

LOCAL 1199

Geriatrics

Wiechowski, Michael, MD

Internal Medicine

Ament, Joseph D., MD
Kadet, Alan, MD
Wiechowski, Michael, MD

LOCAL 32BJ

Cardiology

Mueller, Richard L., MD

Dermatology

Kling, Alan R., MD

Hematology

Frankel, Etta B., MD

Internal Medicine

Ament, Joseph D., MD
Frankel, Etta B., MD
Kadet, Alan, MD
Lutsky, Eric, MD
Mueller, Richard L., MD
Nadel, Lester, MD

Medical Oncology

Frankel, Etta B., MD

MAGNA CARE

Dermatology
Kling, Alan R., MD

Family Practice
Aguero, Jose, MD
Chung, Bruce, MD

Gastroenterology
Attia, Albert, MD
Baiocco, Peter, MD
Zachary, Kirk J., MD

Geriatrics
Kamlet, David A., MD

Hematology
Vizel-Schwartz, Monique, MD

Internal Medicine
Attia, Albert, MD
Baiocco, Peter, MD
Belenkov, Elliot, MD
Glick, Jeffrey, MD
Kamlet, David A., MD
Nadel, Lester, MD
Radin, Allen, MD
Solomon, David Y., MD
Strauss, Steven, MD
Vizel-Schwartz, Monique, MD
Zachary, Kirk J., MD

Medical Oncology
Belenkov, Elliot, MD
Vizel-Schwartz, Monique, MD

OB/GYN
Adler, Alan A., MD

Pediatrics
Weller, Alan S., MD

Physical Medicine & Rehabilitation
Solomon, David Y., MD

Rheumatolgy
Radin, Allen, MD

MANAGED HEALTHCARE

Family Practice
Buchel, Tamara L., MD

MASTERCARE

Internal Medicine
Cohen, Albert, MD

MULTIPLAN

Dermatology
Demar, Leon K., MD

Family Practice
Chung, Bruce, MD
Olmscheid, Bruce, MD
Ravetz, Valerie, MD
Tamarin, Steven, MD

Geriatrics
Kamlet, David A., MD

Hematology
Beautyman, Elizabeth J., MD

Internal Medicine
Beautyman, Elizabeth J., MD
Bendo, Dominick, MD
Bernstein, Stephen J., MD
Blye, Ellen, MD
Charap, Peter, MD

Internal Medicine (cont'd)

Kamlet, David A., MD
Kaufman, David L., MD
Lamm, Steven, MD
Lutsky, Eric, MD
Mellow, Nancy L., MD
Weiner, David J., MD

OB/GYN

Adler, Alan A., MD
Reiss, Ronald J., MD

Pediatrics

Khanna, Kussum, MD
Weller, Alan S., MD

Rheumatolgy

Bernstein, Stephen J., MD

NATIONAL HEALTH PLAN

Internal Medicine

Glick, Jeffrey, MD

NYC CARE

Family Practice

Leeds, Gary, MD
Shepard, Richard, MD

Geriatrics

Schayes, Bernard, MD

Infectious Diseases

Montana, John, MD

Internal Medicine

Bardes, Charles L., MD
Charap, Peter, MD
Kabakow, Bernard, MD

Klein, Susan, MD
Montana, John, MD
Painter, Lucy N., MD
Schayes, Bernard, MD
Solomon, David Y., MD

Medical Oncology

Kabakow, Bernard, MD

OB/GYN

Fischer, Ilene M., MD

Pediatrics

Van Gilder, Max, MD

Physical Medicine & Rehab.

Solomon, David Y., MD

NYL CARE

Internal Medicine

Strauss, Steven, MD

OXFORD

Allergy & Immunology

Falk, George A., MD
Levine, Susan, MD
Lichtenfeld, Amy D., MD

Cardiology

Andersen, Holly S., MD
Graf, Jeffrey H., MD
Kennish, Arthur, MD
Mattes, Leonard, MD
Mueller, Richard L., MD

Critical Care Medicine

Bahr, Gerald S., MD
Konecky, Alan, MD
Posner, David H., MD

Dermatology

Demar, Leon K., MD
Kling, Alan R., MD
Scheiner, Avery M., MD

Emergency Medicine

Isaacs, Daryl M., MD
Lewin, Neal A., MD

Endocrinology

Bernstein, Gerald, MD
Colt, Edward, MD
Merker, Edward, MD

Family Practice

Aguero, Jose, MD
Braun, James F., MD
Buchel, Tamara L., MD
Chung, Bruce, MD
Goldberg, Richard, MD
Horowitz, Mark E., MD
Leeds, Gary, MD
Leichman, Gerald, MD
Levy, Albert, MD
Olmscheid, Bruce, MD
Ravetz, Valerie, MD
Shepard, Richard, MD
Tamarin, Steven, MD

Gastroenterology

Adler, Howard, MD
Arons, Elliot, MD
Attia, Albert, MD
Baiocco, Peter, MD
Brettholz, Edward, MD
Loria, Jeffrey M., MD
Lustbader, Ian, MD
Pearlman, Kenneth I., MD
Weber, Scott, MD
Weintraub, Gerald, MD
Yaffe, Bruce H., MD
Zachary, Kirk J., MD

General Surgery

Cho, Sam K., MD

Geriatrics

Babitz, Lisa E., MD
Bernstein, Donald H., MD
Halper, Peter, MD
Kamlet, David A., MD
Levy, Albert, MD
Mernick, Mitchel, MD

Hematology

Beautyman, Elizabeth J., MD
Buckner, Jeffrey A., MD
Edwards, Colleen A., MD
Frankel, Etta B., MD
Geltman, Richard L., MD
Lewin, Margaret, MD
Vizel-Schwartz, Monique, MD

Infectious Diseases

Bell, Evan T., MD
Fried, Richard P., MD
Levine, Susan, MD

Internal Medicine

Abrams, Robert S., MD
Adler, Howard, MD
Adler, Jack J., MD
Adler, Mitchell A., MD
Amiraian, Richard H., MD
Andersen, Holly S., MD
Arons, Elliot, MD
Attia, Albert, MD
Babitz, Lisa E., MD
Bahr, Gerald S., MD
Baiocco, Peter, MD
Bardes, Charles L., MD
Barnes, Edward, MD
Baskin, David H., MD
Beautyman, Elizabeth J., MD
Beitler, Martin, MD

Internal medicine (cont'd)

Belenkov, Elliot, MD
Bell, Evan T., MD
Bendo, Dominick, MD
Bernstein, Donald H., MD
Bernstein, Gerald, MD
Bernstein, Stephen J., MD
Blye, Ellen, MD
Brandon, Donald E., MD
Bregman, Zachary, MD
Brettholz, Edward, MD
Bruno, Peter J., MD
Buckner, Jeffrey A., MD
Burns, Margaret M., MD
Charap, Peter, MD
Cohen, Albert, MD
Cohen, Robert L., MD
Colt, Edward, MD
Diamond, Carol, MD
Edwards, Colleen A., MD
Falk, George A., MD
Fallick, Nina, MD
Frankel, Etta B., MD
Fried, Richard P., MD
Friedman, Jeffrey P., MD
Furman, Alice, MD
Geltman, Richard L., MD
Glick, Jeffrey, MD
Golden, Flavia A., MD
Graf, Jeffrey H., MD
Grossman, Howard A., MD
Halper, Peter, MD
Hammer, David, MD
Hauptman, Allen S., MD
Horbar, Gary, MD
Isaacs, Daryl M., MD
Kabakow, Bernard, MD
Kamlet, David A., MD
Kaufman, David L., MD
Keller, Raymond S., MD
Kennedy, James T., MD
Kennish, Arthur, MD

Klein, Susan, MD
Konecky, Alan, MD
Kramer, Sara, MD
Lamm, Steven, MD
Leventhal, Gerald H., MD
Levine, Susan, MD
Lewin, Margaret, MD
Lewin, Neal A., MD
Lichtenfeld, Amy D., MD
Loria, Jeffrey M., MD
Lustbader, Ian, MD
Lutsky, Eric, MD
Mattes, Leonard, MD
Merker, Edward, MD
Mernick, Mitchel, MD
Moyer, Lawson, MD
Mueller, Richard L., MD
Nadel, Lester, MD
Nicolaides, Maria N., MD
Painter, Lucy N., MD
Palumbo, Michael J., MD
Pearlman, Kenneth I., MD
Perskin, Michael, MD
Pitaro, Gregory, MD
Posner, David H., MD
Radin, Allen, MD
Ruden, Ronald, MD
Schwartz, Lawrence P., MD
Shay, William E., MD
Strauss, Steven, MD
Suozzi, William, MD
Underberg, James A., MD
Vizel-Schwartz, Monique, MD
Weber, Scott, MD
Weiner, David J., MD
Weinstein, Melvin, MD
Weintraub, Gerald, MD
Weiser, Frank M., MD
Weiss, Nancy L., MD
Woronoff, Richard S., MD
Yaffe, Bruce H., MD
Young, Kevin S., MD
Zachary, Kirk J., MD

Medical Oncology

Belenkov, Elliot, MD
Buckner, Jeffrey A., MD
Diamond, Carol, MD
Frankel, Etta B., MD
Geltman, Richard L., MD
Kabakow, Bernard, MD
Lewin, Margaret, MD
Mernick, Mitchel, MD
Vizel-Schwartz, Monique, MD

Nephrology

Nicolaides, Maria N., MD

OB/GYN

Adler, Alan A., MD
Berman, Alvin, MD
Brodman, Michael, MD
Corio, Laura, MD
Fischer, Ilene M., MD
Friedman, Lynn, MD
Goldman, Gary H., MD
Gruss, Leslie, MD
Ho, Alison, MD
Lebowitz, Nancy, MD
Nachamie, Rebecca, MD
Park, Brian, MD
Reiss, Ronald J., MD
Zilberstein, Inga, MD

Pediatric Allergy & Immunology

Lazarus, Herbert, MD

Pediatric Endocrinology

Rosenbaum, Michael, MD

Pediatric Rheumatology

Lazarus, Herbert, MD

Pediatrics

Coffey, Robert J., MD
Goldstein, Judith, MD

Grunfeld, Paul, MD
Kahn, Max A., MD
Kessler, Ruth E., MD
Khanna, Kussum, MD
Lazarus, Herbert, MD
Pasquariello, Palmo, MD
Rosenbaum, Michael, MD
Rosenfeld, Suzanne, MD
Spielman, Gerald, MD
Sussman, Elihu, MD
Van Gilder, Max, MD
Weller, Alan S., MD
Wishnick, Marcia M., MD

Pulmonology

Abrams, Robert S., MD
Adler, Jack J., MD
Bregman, Zachary, MD
Falk, George A., MD
Hammer, David, MD
Keller, Raymond S., MD
Konecky, Alan, MD
Posner, David H., MD
Schwartz, Lawrence P., MD
Woronoff, Richard S., MD

Rheumatolgy

Bernstein, Donald H., MD
Bernstein, Stephen J., MD
Kramer, Sara, MD
Leventhal, Gerald H., MD
Radin, Allen, MD

PHS/GUARDIAN

Allergy & Immunology

Levine, Susan, MD

Cardiology

Graf, Jeffrey H., MD
Mueller, Richard L., MD

Critical Care Medicine

Konecky, Alan, MD

Dermatology

Kling, Alan R., MD
Scheiner, Avery M., MD

Family Practice

Aguero, Jose, MD
Chung, Bruce, MD
Horowitz, Mark E., MD
Olmscheid, Bruce, MD
Ravetz, Valerie, MD
Tamarin, Steven, MD

Gastroenterology

Baiocco, Peter, MD
Brettholz, Edward, MD
Goldberg, Edward S., MD
Loria, Jeffrey M., MD
Pearlman, Kenneth I., MD
Weintraub, Gerald, MD
Zachary, Kirk J., MD

Geriatrics

Babitz, Lisa E., MD
Mernick, Mitchel, MD

Hematology

Buckner, Jeffrey A., MD
Geltman, Richard L., MD
Lewin, Margaret, MD

Infectious Diseases

Fisher, Laura, MD
Levine, Susan, MD
Wallach, Jeffrey, MD

Internal Medicine

Abrams, Robert S., MD
Adler, Jack J., MD
Babitz, Lisa E., MD
Baiocco, Peter, MD
Baskin, David H., MD

Brandon, Donald E., MD
Brettholz, Edward, MD
Buckner, Jeffrey A., MD
Charap, Peter, MD
Cohen, Albert, MD
Diamond, Carol, MD
Fisher, Laura, MD
Geltman, Richard L., MD
Goldberg, Edward S., MD
Golden, Flavia A., MD
Graf, Jeffrey H., MD
Grossman, Howard A., MD
Hurd, Beverly, MD
Kadet, Alan, MD
Kaufman, David L., MD
Keller, Raymond S., MD
Konecky, Alan, MD
Kramer, Sara, MD
Levine, Susan, MD
Lewin, Margaret, MD
Loria, Jeffrey M., MD
Mernick, Mitchel, MD
Mueller, Richard L., MD
Nicolaides, Maria N., MD
Pearlman, Kenneth I., MD
Radin, Allen, MD
Schwartz, Lawrence P., MD
Shay, William E., MD
Strauss, Steven, MD
Suozzi, William, MD
Wallach, Jeffrey, MD
Weinstein, Melvin, MD
Weintraub, Gerald, MD
Weiser, Frank M., MD
Woronoff, Richard S., MD
Zachary, Kirk J., MD

Medical Oncology

Buckner, Jeffrey A., MD
Diamond, Carol, MD
Geltman, Richard L., MD
Lewin, Margaret, MD
Mernick, Mitchel, MD

Nephrology
Nicolaides, Maria N., MD

OB/GYN
Adler, Alan A., MD
Reiss, Ronald J., MD
Zilberstein, Inga, MD

Pediatrics
Coffey, Robert J., MD
Grunfeld, Paul, MD
Khanna, Kussum, MD
Sussman, Elihu, MD
Van Gilder, Max, MD
Weller, Alan S., MD

Pulmonology
Abrams, Robert S., MD
Adler, Jack J., MD
Keller, Raymond S., MD
Konecky, Alan, MD
Schwartz, Lawrence P., MD
Woronoff, Richard S., MD

Rheumatolgy
Kramer, Sara, MD
Radin, Allen, MD

POS

Internal Medicine
Bruno, Peter J., MD

PREMIER PREFERRED

Internal Medicine
Bernstein, Stephen J., MD
Charap, Peter, MD
Fallick, Nina, MD

OB/GYN
Adler, Alan A., MD
Berman, Alvin, MD

Rheumatolgy
Bernstein, Stephen J., MD

PRIVATE HEALTH CARE

Allergy & Immunology
Falk, George A., MD

Cardiology
Kennish, Arthur, MD

Dermatology
Demar, Leon K., MD
Kling, Alan R., MD
Scheiner, Avery M., MD

Emergency Medicine
Isaacs, Daryl M., MD

Family Practice
Aguero, Jose, MD
Chung, Bruce, MD
Horowitz, Mark E., MD
Olmscheid, Bruce, MD
Ravetz, Valerie, MD
Tamarin, Steven, MD

Gastroenterology
Attia, Albert, MD
Baiocco, Peter, MD
Brettholz, Edward, MD
Loria, Jeffrey M., MD
Weber, Scott, MD
Weintraub, Gerald, MD
Yaffe, Bruce H., MD
Zachary, Kirk J., MD

Geriatrics
Kamlet, David A., MD

Hematology
Buckner, Jeffrey A., MD
Vizel-Schwartz, Monique, MD

Infectious Diseases
Fisher, Laura, MD

Internal Medicine
Adler, Jack J., MD
Attia, Albert, MD
Baiocco, Peter, MD
Bardes, Charles L., MD
Bernstein, Stephen J., MD
Brettholz, Edward, MD
Buckner, Jeffrey A., MD
Charap, Peter, MD
Cohen, Robert L., MD
Falk, George A., MD
Fisher, Laura, MD
Golden, Flavia A., MD
Isaacs, Daryl M., MD
Kabakow, Bernard, MD
Kamlet, David A., MD
Kaufman, David L., MD
Kennish, Arthur, MD
Klein, Susan, MD
Loria, Jeffrey M., MD
Lutsky, Eric, MD
Nadel, Lester, MD
Nicolaides, Maria N., MD
Shay, William E., MD
Suozzi, William, MD
Vizel-Schwartz, Monique, MD
Weber, Scott, MD
Weinstein, Melvin, MD
Weintraub, Gerald, MD
Weiser, Frank M., MD
Woronoff, Richard S., MD
Yaffe, Bruce H., MD
Zachary, Kirk J., MD

Medical Oncology
Buckner, Jeffrey A., MD
Kabakow, Bernard, MD
Vizel-Schwartz, Monique, MD

Nephrology
Nicolaides, Maria N., MD

OB/GYN
Adler, Alan A., MD
Berman, Alvin, MD
Fischer, Ilene M., MD
Goldman, Gary H., MD
Gruss, Leslie, MD
Hobgood, Laura S., MD
Lebowitz, Nancy, MD
Park, Brian, MD

Pediatrics
Coffey, Robert J., MD
Goldstein, Judith, MD
Grunfeld, Paul, MD
Khanna, Kussum, MD
Pasquariello, Palmo, MD
Van Gilder, Max, MD
Weller, Alan S., MD

Pulmonology
Adler, Jack J., MD
Falk, George A., MD
Woronoff, Richard S., MD

Rheumatolgy
Bernstein, Stephen J., MD

PRU CARE

Allergy & Immunology
Lichtenfeld, Amy D., MD

Critical Care Medicine

Konecky, Alan, MD

Family Practice

Chung, Bruce, MD
Levy, Albert, MD
Ravetz, Valerie, MD

Gastroenterology

Attia, Albert, MD
Brettholz, Edward, MD
Loria, Jeffrey M., MD
Weintraub, Gerald, MD

Geriatrics

Babitz, Lisa E., MD
Bernstein, Donald H., MD
Levy, Albert, MD

Hematology

Frankel, Etta B., MD
Vizel-Schwartz, Monique, MD

Infectious Diseases

Fried, Richard P., MD

Internal Medicine

Adler, Jack J., MD
Attia, Albert, MD
Babitz, Lisa E., MD
Baskin, David H., MD
Belenkov, Elliot, MD
Bernstein, Donald H., MD
Brettholz, Edward, MD
Cohen, Robert L., MD
Frankel, Etta B., MD
Fried, Richard P., MD
Kabakow, Bernard, MD
Kaufman, David L., MD
Kennedy, James T., MD
Konecky, Alan, MD
Kramer, Sara, MD
Leventhal, Gerald H., MD

Lichtenfeld, Amy D., MD
Loria, Jeffrey M., MD
Vizel-Schwartz, Monique, MD
Weintraub, Gerald, MD
Woronoff, Richard S., MD

Medical Oncology

Belenkov, Elliot, MD
Frankel, Etta B., MD
Kabakow, Bernard, MD
Vizel-Schwartz, Monique, MD

OB/GYN

Berman, Alvin, MD
Fischer, Ilene M., MD
Gruss, Leslie, MD
Hobgood, Laura S., MD
Park, Brian, MD
Zilberstein, Inga, MD

Pediatrics

Grunfeld, Paul, MD
Kessler, Ruth E., MD
Khanna, Kussum, MD
Van Gilder, Max, MD
Wishnick, Marcia M., MD

Pulmonology

Adler, Jack J., MD
Konecky, Alan, MD
Woronoff, Richard S., MD

Rheumatolgy

Bernstein, Donald H., MD
Kramer, Sara, MD
Leventhal, Gerald H., MD

SANUS

Family Practice

Goldberg, Richard, MD

Gastroenterology

Brettholz, Edward, MD

Internal Medicine

Adler, Jack J., MD
Brettholz, Edward, MD
Weiner, David J., MD
Woronoff, Richard S., MD

Pulmonology

Adler, Jack J., MD
Woronoff, Richard S., MD

SELECT PROVIDERS

Internal Medicine

Charap, Peter, MD

UNIFIED

Cardiology

Kennish, Arthur, MD

Family Practice

Goldberg, Richard, MD
Shepard, Richard, MD

Gastroenterology

Yaffe, Bruce H., MD

Geriatrics

Kamlet, David A., MD

Hematology

Buckner, Jeffrey A., MD
Vizel-Schwartz, Monique, MD

Infectious Diseases

Fisher, Laura, MD

Internal Medicine

Ament, Joseph D., MD
Bardes, Charles L., MD
Buckner, Jeffrey A., MD
Fallick, Nina, MD
Fisher, Laura, MD
Kamlet, David A., MD
Kennish, Arthur, MD
Underberg, James A., MD
Vizel-Schwartz, Monique, MD
Weiner, David J., MD
Yaffe, Bruce H., MD

Medical Oncology

Buckner, Jeffrey A., MD
Vizel-Schwartz, Monique, MD

UNITED HEALTHCARE

Allergy & Immunology

Lichtenfeld, Amy D., MD

Cardiology

Graf, Jeffrey H., MD
Mueller, Richard L., MD

Critical Care Medicine

Bahr, Gerald S., MD
Konecky, Alan, MD
Posner, David H., MD

Dermatology

Demar, Leon K., MD
Scheiner, Avery M., MD

Emergency Medicine

Isaacs, Daryl M., MD

Family Practice

Buchel, Tamara L., MD
Goldberg, Richard, MD
Levy, Albert, MD
Shepard, Richard, MD

Gastroenterology

Brettholz, Edward, MD
Loria, Jeffrey M., MD
Lustbader, Ian, MD
Pearlman, Kenneth I., MD
Weber, Scott, MD

Geriatrics

Goodman, Karl, MD
Kamlet, David A., MD
Levy, Albert, MD
Mernick, Mitchel, MD
Wiechowski, Michael, MD

Hematology

Frankel, Etta B., MD

Infectious Diseases

Bell, Evan T., MD
Fisher, Laura, MD
Fried, Richard P., MD

Internal Medicine

Bahr, Gerald S., MD
Barnes, Edward, MD
Baskin, David H., MD
Belenkov, Elliot, MD
Bell, Evan T., MD
Bernstein, Stephen J., MD
Brandon, Donald E., MD
Bregman, Zachary, MD
Brettholz, Edward, MD
Bruno, Peter J., MD
Charap, Peter, MD
Cohen, Albert, MD
Cohen, Robert L., MD
Dhalla, Satish, MD
Fisher, Laura, MD
Frankel, Etta B., MD
Fried, Richard P., MD
Friedman, Jeffrey P., MD
Furman, Alice, MD
Goodman, Karl, MD

Graf, Jeffrey H., MD
Isaacs, Daryl M., MD
Kadet, Alan, MD
Kamlet, David A., MD
Kaufman, David L., MD
Klein, Susan, MD
Konecky, Alan, MD
Kramer, Sara, MD
Lamm, Steven, MD
Leventhal, Gerald H., MD
Lichtenfeld, Amy D., MD
Loria, Jeffrey M., MD
Lustbader, Ian, MD
Mernick, Mitchel, MD
Moyer, Lawson, MD
Mueller, Richard L., MD
Nadel, Lester, MD
Painter, Lucy N., MD
Palumbo, Michael J., MD
Pearlman, Kenneth I., MD
Pitaro, Gregory, MD
Posner, David H., MD
Radin, Allen, MD
Ruden, Ronald, MD
Schwartz, Lawrence P., MD
Shay, William E., MD
Solomon, David Y., MD
Strauss, Steven, MD
Suozzi, William, MD
Weber, Scott, MD
Weinstein, Melvin, MD
Wiechowski, Michael, MD

Medical Oncology

Belenkov, Elliot, MD
Frankel, Etta B., MD
Mernick, Mitchel, MD

OB/GYN

Adler, Alan A., MD
Gruss, Leslie, MD
Lebowitz, Nancy, MD
Park, Brian, MD
Zilberstein, Inga, MD

Pediatrics

Goldstein, Judith, MD
Grunfeld, Paul, MD
Kessler, Ruth E., MD
Pasquariello, Palmo, MD
Sussman, Elihu, MD
Weller, Alan S., MD

Physical Medicine & Rehabilitation

Solomon, David Y., MD

Pulmonology

Bregman, Zachary, MD
Konecky, Alan, MD
Posner, David H., MD
Schwartz, Lawrence P., MD

Rheumatolgy

Bernstein, Stephen J., MD
Kramer, Sara, MD
Leventhal, Gerald H., MD
Radin, Allen, MD

Language Index

AFRIKKAANS

OB/GYN
Berman, Alvin, MD

Pediatrics
Stein, Barry, B., MD

ALBANIAN

Pediatrics
Kahn, Max, A., MD

ARABIC

Internal Medicine
Solomon, David, Y., MD

OB/GYN
Livoti, Carol, MD
Sassoon, Albert, K., MD, MPH
Sillay, Laila, R., MD

Physical Medicine & Rehabilitation
Solomon, David, Y., MD

CAMBODIAN

Endocrinology
Bernstein, Gerald, MD

Internal Medicine
Bernstein, Gerald, MD

CANTONESE

Critical Care Medicine
Konecky, Alan, MD

Internal Medicine
Konecky, Alan, MD

Pulmonology
Konecky, Alan, MD

CHINESE

Family Practice
Chung, Bruce, MD

Internal Medicine
Golden, Flavia, A., MD

CREOLE

Internal Medicine
Furman, Alice, MD

DUTCH

Critical Care Medicine
Posner, David H., MD

Internal Medicine
Abrams, Robert S., MD
Posner, David H., MD

Pulmonology
Abrams, Robert S., MD
Posner, David H., MD

FRENCH

Cardiology
Andersen, Holly S., MD
Franklin, Kenneth W., MD

Critical Care Medicine
Posner, David H., MD

Dermatology
Kling, Alan R., MD

Emergency Medicine
Isaacs, Daryl M, MD
Lewin, Neal A, MD

Family Practice
Horowitz, Mark E., MD
Levy, Albert, MD

Gastroenterology
Altman, Kenneth A., MD
Baiocco, Peter, MD

General Practice
Shapiro, Irene, MD

Geriatrics
Levy, Albert, MD
Schayes, Bernard, MD

Gynecology
Beitner, Orit, MD

FRENCH

Hematology
Vizel-Schwartz, Monique, MD

Infectious Diseases
Fisher, Laura, MD
Fried, Richard P., MD

Internal Medicine
Abrams, Robert S., MD
Altman, Kenneth A., MD
Andersen, Holly S., MD
Baiocco, Peter, MD
Bendo, Dominick, MD
Fisher, Laura, MD
Franklin, Kenneth W., MD
Fried, Richard P., MD
Golden, Flavia A., MD
Horovitz, H. Leonard, MD
Hurd, Beverly, MD
Isaacs, Daryl M., MD
Kaufman, David L., MD
Lewin, Neal A., MD
Mellow, Nancy L., MD
Posner, David H., MD
Rodman, John S., MD
Schayes, Bernard, MD
Solomon, David Y., MD
Vizel-Schwartz, Monique, MD

Medical Oncology
Vizel-Schwartz, Monique, MD

Nephrology
Rodman, John S., MD

OB/GYN
Bello, Gaetano, MD
Livoti, Carol, MD
Reiss, Ronald J., MD
Sassoon, Albert K., MD, MPH
Sillay, Laila R., MD

Pediatric Allergy & Immunology
Lazarus, Herbert, MD

Pediatric Rheumatology
Lazarus, Herbert, MD

Pediatrics
Goldstein, Judith, MD
Kahn, Max A., MD
Lazarus, Herbert, MD
Wishnick, Marcia, M, MD

Physical Medicine & Rehabilitation
Solomon, David Y, MD

Pulmonology
Abrams, Robert S, MD
Horovitz, H. Leonard, MD
Posner, David H., MD

GAELIC

Endocrinology
Bernstein, Gerald, MD

Internal Medicine
Bernstein, Gerald, MD

GERMAN

Cardiology
Andersen, Holly S., MD
Graf, Jeffrey H., MD

Gastroenterology
Altman, Kenneth A., MD

Internal Medicine
Altman, Kenneth A., MD
Andersen, Holly S., MD
Cohen, Albert, MD
Graf, Jeffrey H., MD
Horovitz, H. Leonard, MD
Lamm, Steven, MD
Solomon, David Y., MD
Weiser, Frank M., MD

Pediatrics
Goldstein, Judith, MD
Grunfeld, Paul, MD
Kessler, Ruth E., MD

Physical Medicine & Rehabilitation
Solomon, David, Y, MD

Pulmonology
Horovitz, H. Leonard, MD

GREEK

Cardiology
Mueller, Richard L., MD

Internal Medicine
Glick, Jeffrey, MD
Mueller, Richard L., MD
Nicolaides, Maria N., MD

Nephrology
Nicolaides, Maria N., MD

Pediatrics
Wishnick, Marcia M., MD

HEBREW

Emergency Medicine
Isaacs, Daryl M., MD

Gastroenterology
Altman, Kenneth A., MD

Geriatrics
Kamlet, David A., MD
Mernick, Mitchel, MD

Gynecology
Beitner, Orit, MD

Infectious Diseases
Fisher, Laura, MD

Internal Medicine
Altman, Kenneth A., MD
Fisher, Laura, MD
Isaacs, Daryl M., MD
Kamlet, David A., MD
Mernick, Mitchel, MD

Medical Oncology
Mernick, Mitchel, MD

OB/GYN
Gruss, Leslie, MD
Wenger, Judith, MD

Pediatrics
Stein, Barry B., MD

HINDI

Pediatrics
Khanna, Kussum, MD

HUNGARIAN

Cardiology
Mueller, Richard L., MD

Internal Medicine
Klein, Susan, MD
Mueller, Richard L., MD

Pediatrics
Grunfeld, Paul, MD

ITALIAN

Critical Care Medicine
Bahr, Gerald S., MD

Posner, David H., MD

Emergency Medicine
Isaacs, Daryl M., MD

Family Practice
Aguero, Jose, MD

Gastroenterology
Baiocco, Peter, MD

Internal Medicine
Bahr, Gerald S., MD
Baiocco, Peter, MD
Bendo, Dominick, MD
Bernstein, Stephen J., MD
Blye, Ellen, MD
Bruno, Peter J., MD
Cohen, Albert, MD
Glick, Jeffrey, MD
Isaacs, Daryl M., MD
Lamm, Steven, MD
Posner, David H., MD

OB/GYN
Bello, Gaetano, MD
Creatura, Chris, MD
Nachamie, Rebecca, MD
Zilberstein, Inga, MD

Pediatrics
Goldstein, Judith, MD
Pasquariello, Palmo, MD
Wishnick, Marcia M., MD

Pulmonology
Posner, David H., MD

Rheumatolgy
Bernstein, Stephen J., MD

JAPANESE

Family Practice
Chung, Bruce, MD

General Surgery
Cho, Sam K., MD

KOREAN

General Surgery
Cho, Sam K., MD

MANDARIN

Critical Care Medicine
Konecky, Alan, MD

Internal Medicine
Konecky, Alan, MD

Pulmonology
Konecky, Alan, MD

PERSIAN

Internal Medicine
Solomon, David Y., MD

**Physical Medicine
& Rehabilitation**
Solomon, David Y., MD

POLISH

Internal Medicine
Lamm, Steven, MD
Weiser, Frank M., MD

OB/GYN
Nachamie, Rebecca, MD

PORTUGESE

Family Practice
Leeds, Gary, MD
Levy, Albert, MD

Geriatrics
Levy, Albert, MD

Internal Medicine
Langelier, Carolyn A., MD

ROMANIAN

Cardiology
Andersen, Holly S., MD

Endocrinology
Merker, Edward, MD

Internal Medicine
Andersen, Holly S., MD
Merker, Edward, MD

RUSSIAN

Allergy & Immunology
Falk, George A., MD

Family Practice
Aguero, Jose, MD
Leichman, Gerald, MD

Gastroenterology
Dubin, Richard, MD

Geriatrics
Mernick, Mitchel, MD

Gynecology

Beitner, Orit, MD

Internal Medicine

Belenkov, Elliot, MD
Bernstein, Stephen J., MD
Dubin, Richard, MD
Falk, George A., MD
Mernick, Mitchel, MD

Medical Oncology

Belenkov, Elliot, MD
Mernick, Mitchel, MD

OB/GYN

Zilberstein, Inga, MD

Pediatrics

Wishnick, Marcia M., MD

Pulmonology

Falk, George A., MD

Rheumatolgy

Bernstein, Stephen J., MD

SPANISH

Allergy & Immunology

Falk, George A., MD
Levine, Susan, MD
Lichtenfeld, Amy D., MD

Cardiology

Andersen, Holly S., MD
Graf, Jeffrey H., MD
Kennish, Arthur, MD
Mattes, Leonard, MD
Mueller, Richard L., MD

Critical Care Medicine

Bahr, Gerald S., MD

Konecky, Alan, MD
Posner, David H., MD

Dermatology

Demar, Leon K., MD
Kling, Alan R., MD

Emergency Medicine

Isaacs, Daryl M., MD
Lewin, Neal A., MD

Endocrinology

Bernstein, Gerald, MD
Colt, Edward, MD
Merker, Edward, MD

Family Practice

Aguero, Jose, MD
Braun, James F., MD
Buchel, Tamara L., MD
Clements, Jerry, MD
Goldberg, Richard, MD
Horowitz, Mark E., MD
Leeds, Gary, MD
Leichman, Gerald, MD
Levy, Albert, MD
Olmscheid, Bruce, MD
Shepard, Richard, MD
Tamarin, Steven, MD

Gastroenterology

Altman, Kenneth A., MD
Arons, Elliot, MD
Attia, Albert, MD
Baiocco, Peter, MD
Bearnot, Robert, MD
Brettholz, Edward, MD
Goldberg, Edward S., MD
Loria, Jeffrey M., MD
Lustbader, Ian, MD
Present, Daniel H., MD
Weber, Scott, MD

General Practice

Shapiro, Irene, MD

Geriatrics

Bernstein, Donald H., MD
Goodman, Karl, MD
Halper, Peter, MD
Kamlet, David A., MD
Levy, Albert, MD
Mernick, Mitchel, MD
Schayes, Bernard, MD
Wiechowski, Michael, MD

Gynecology

Beitner, Orit, MD
Berman, Joan K., MD

Hematology

Buckner, Jeffrey A., MD
Edwards, Colleen A., MD
Frankel, Etta, B., MD
Geltman, Richard L., MD
Vizel-Schwartz, Monique, MD

Infectious Diseases

Gale, Robert K., MD
Levine, Susan, MD
Montana, John, MD
Rudin, Debra, MD
Silverman, David, MD

Internal Medicine

Abrams, Robert S., MD
Altman, Kenneth A., MD
Ament, Joseph D., MD
Andersen, Holly S., MD
Arons, Elliot, MD
Attia, Albert, MD
Bahr, Gerald S., MD
Baiocco, Peter, MD
Barnes, Edward, MD
Baskin, David H., MD
Bearnot, Robert, MD

Belenkov, Elliot, MD
Bendo, Dominick, MD
Bernstein, Donald H., MD
Bernstein, Gerald, MD
Bernstein, Stephen J., MD
Blye, Ellen, MD
Brandon, Donald E., MD
Brettholz, Edward, MD
Bruno, Peter J., MD
Buckner, Jeffrey A., MD
Burns, Margaret M., MD
Charap, Peter, MD
Cohen, Albert, MD
Cohen, Robert L., MD
Colt, Edward, MD
De Cotis, Sue Gene, MD
Diamond, Carol, MD
Edwards, Colleen A., MD
Falk, George A., MD
Frankel, Etta B., MD
Friedman, Jeffrey P., MD
Furman, Alice, MD
Gale, Robert K., MD
Geltman, Richard L., MD
Glick, Jeffrey, MD
Goldberg, Edward S., MD
Golden, Flavia A., MD
Goodman, Karl, MD
Graf, Jeffrey H., MD
Halper, Peter, MD
Hammer, David, MD
Higgins, Lawrence A., DO,
Horbar, Gary, MD
Isaacs, Daryl M., MD
Kabakow, Bernard, MD
Kadet, Alan, MD
Kamlet, David A., MD
Kaufman, David L., MD
Keller, Raymond S., MD
Kennedy, James T., MD
Kennish, Arthur, MD
Konecky, Alan, MD
Kramer, Sara, MD

Internal Medicine (cont'd)

Lamm, Steven, MD
Langelier, Carolyn A., MD
Levine, Susan, MD
Lewin, Neal A., MD
Lichtenfeld, Amy D., MD
Loria, Jeffrey M., MD
Lustbader, Ian, MD
Lutsky, Eric, MD
Mattes, Leonard, MD
Mellow, Nancy L., MD
Merker, Edward, MD
Mernick, Mitchel, MD
Montana, John, MD
Mueller, Richard L., MD
Nadel, Lester, MD
Nicolaides, Maria N., MD
Perskin, Michael, MD
Posner, David, H, MD
Present, Daniel H., MD
Rodman, John S., MD
Rooney, Ellen, MD
Ruden, Ronald, MD
Rudin, Debra, MD
Schayes, Bernard, MD
Shay, William E., MD
Silverman, David, MD
Solomon, David, Y, MD
Strauss, Steven, MD
Suozzi, William, MD
Vizel-Schwartz, Monique, MD
Weber, Scott, MD
Weinstein, Melvin, MD
Weiser, Frank M., MD
Wiechowski, Michael, MD
Young, Kevin S., MD

Medical Oncology

Belenkov, Elliot, MD
Buckner, Jeffrey A., MD
Diamond, Carol, MD

Frankel, Etta B., MD
Geltman, Richard L., MD
Kabakow, Bernard, MD
Mernick, Mitchel, MD
Vizel-Schwartz, Monique, MD

Nephrology

Nicolaides, Maria N., MD
Rodman, John S., MD

OB/GYN

Adler, Alan A., MD
Bello, Gaetano, MD
Berman, Alvin, MD
Brodman, Michael, MD
Carlon, Anne, MD
Cavalli, Adele, MD
Chin Quee, Karlene, MD
Corio, Laura, MD
Creatura, Chris, MD
Fischer, Ilene M., MD
Goldman, Gary H., MD
Gruss, Leslie, MD
Ho, Alison, MD
Lebowitz, Nancy, MD
Livoti, Carol, MD
Nachamie, Rebecca, MD
Park, Brian, MD
Reiss, Ronald J., MD
Sassoon, Albert K., MD, MPH
Sillay, Laila R., MD
Wenger, Judith, MD
Zilberstein, Inga, MD

Pediatric Allergy & Immunology

Lazarus, Herbert, MD

Pediatric Endocrinology

Rosenbaum, Michael, MD

Pediatric Pulmonology

Elbirt-Bender, Paula, MD

Pediatric Rheumatology
Lazarus, Herbert, MD

Pediatrics
Elbirt-Bender, Paula, MD
Grunfeld, Paul, MD
Kahn, Max A., MD
Khanna, Kussum, MD
Lazarus, Herbert, MD
Lantz, Howard, MD
Murphy, Ramon J. C., MD
Pasquariello, Palmo, MD
Rosenbaum, Michael, MD
Rosenfeld, Suzanne, MD
Seed, Wm, MD
Spielman, Gerald, MD
Stein, Barry B., MD
Van, Gilder, Max, MD
Weller, Alan S., MD
Wishnick, Marcia M., MD

Physical Medicine & Rehabilitation
Solomon, David Y., MD

Pulmonology
Abrams, Robert S., MD
Falk, George A., MD
Hammer, David, MD
Keller, Raymond S., MD
Konecky, Alan, MD
Posner, David H., MD

Rheumatolgy
Bernstein, Donald H., MD
Bernstein, Stephen J., MD
Kramer, Sara, MD

TAGALOG

Hematology
Buckner, Jeffrey A., MD

Internal Medicine
Buckner, Jeffrey A., MD
Klein, Susan, MD
Weiser, Frank M., MD

Medical Oncology
Buckner, Jeffrey A., MD

OB/GYN
Reiss, Ronald J., MD

YIDDISH

Cardiology
Graf, Jeffrey H., MD

Gastroenterology
Altman, Kenneth A., MD
Weintraub, Gerald, MD

Geriatrics
Mernick, Mitchel, MD

Internal Medicine
Altman, Kenneth A., MD
Graf, Jeffrey H., MD
Kabakow, Bernard, MD
Mernick, Mitchel, MD
Weintraub, Gerald, MD

Medical Oncology
Kabakow, Bernard, MD
Mernick, Mitchel, MD

Pediatric Pulmonology
Elbirt-Bender, Paula, MD

Pediatrics
Elbirt-Bender, Paula, MD

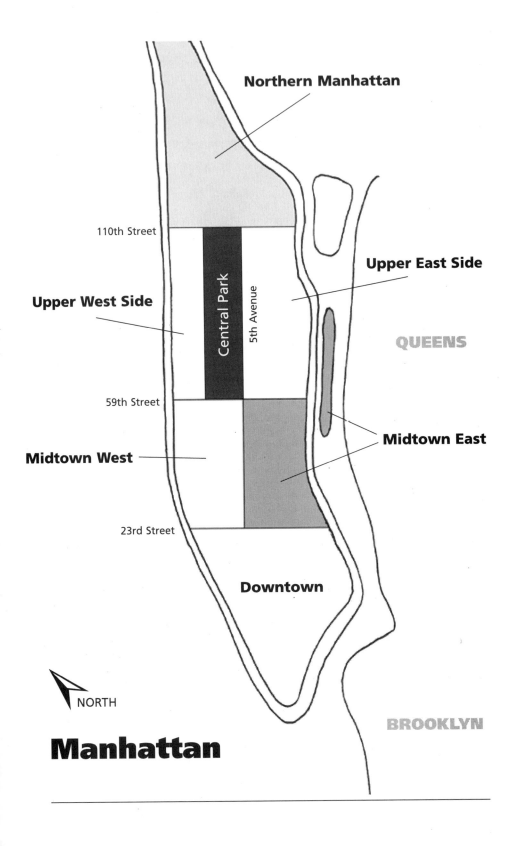

Northern Manhattan

110th Street

Upper East Side

Upper West Side

Central Park

5th Avenue

QUEENS

59th Street

Midtown West

Midtown East

23rd Street

Downtown

NORTH

BROOKLYN

Manhattan

Location

DOWNTOWN DOCTORS

Emergency Medicine

Isaacs, Daryl M., MD

Family Practice

Braun, James F., MD
Clements, Jerry, MD
Goldberg, Richard, MD
Horowitz, Mark E., MD
Leeds, Gary, MD
Olmscheid, Bruce, MD

Geriatrics

Bernstein, Donald H., MD
Brettholz, Edward, MD
Halper, Peter, MD

Hematology

Vizel-Schwartz, Monique, MD

Internal Medicine

Beitler, Martin, MD
Bernstein, Donald H., MD
Brettholz, Edward, MD
Burns, Margaret M., MD
Cohen, Robert L., MD
Dellosso, John, MD
Dhalla, Satish, MD
Grossman, Howard A., MD

Halper, Peter, MD
Hammer, David, MD
Higgins, Lawrence A., DO, MPH
Isaacs, Daryl M., MD
Kabakow, Bernard, MD
Kaufman, David L., MD
Mellow, Nancy L., MD
Montana, John, MD
Shay, William E., MD
Vizel-Schwartz, Monique, MD
Wallach, Jeffrey, MD
Woronoff, Richard S., MD

Medical Oncology

Kabakow, Bernard, MD
Vizel-Schwartz, Monique, MD

OB/GYN

Cavalli, Adele, MD
Gruss, Leslie, MD

Pediatrics

Coffey, Robert J., MD
Hammer, David, MD
Sussman, Elihu, MD
Woronoff, Richard S, MD

Rheumatolgy

Bernstein, Donald H., MD

MIDTOWN EAST DOCTORS

Cardiology
Mueller, Richard L., MD

Critical Care Medicine
Bahr, Gerald S., MD

Dermatology
Long, Willam T., Dr.

Emergency Medicine
Lewin, Neal A., MD

Endocrinology
Park, Constance, MD

Family Practice
Buchel, Tamara L., MD
Chung, Bruce, MD
Leichman, Gerald, MD
Ravetz, Valerie, MD

Gastroenterology
Adler, Howard, MD
Bearnot, Robert, MD
Dubin, Richard, MD
Lustbader, Ian, MD
Pearlman, Kenneth I., MD
Weber, Scott, MD
Zachary, Kirk J., MD

General Surgery
Cho, Sam K., MD

Geriatrics
Mernick, Mitchel, MD

Hematology
Buckner, Jeffrey A., MD
Udesky, Robert A., MD

Infectious Diseases
Bell, Evan T., MD
Gale, Robert K., MD
Rudin, Debra, MD

Internal Medicine
Adler, Howard, MD
Adler, Mitchell A., MD
Bahr, Gerald S., MD
Barnes, Edward, MD
Bearnot, Robert, MD
Bell, Evan T., MD
Bregman, Zachary, MD
Bruno, Peter J., MD
Buckner, Jeffrey A., MD
De Cotis, Sue Gene, MD
Dubin, Richard, MD
Friedman, Jeffrey P., MD
Gale, Robert K., MD
Hauptman, Allen S., MD
Kennedy, James T., MD
Kramer, Sara, MD
Langelier, Carolyn A., MD
Lewin, Neal A., MD
Lustbader, Ian, MD
Lutsky, Eric, MD
Mernick, Mitchel, MD
Mueller, Richard L., MD
Nadel, Lester, MD
Newman, Mark R., MD
Palumbo, Michael J., MD
Park, Constance, MD
Pearlman, Kenneth I., MD
Perskin, Michael, MD
Pitaro, Gregory, MD
Rodman, John S., MD
Rudin, Debra, MD
Schwartz, Lawrence P, MD
Strauss, Steven, MD
Udesky, Robert A., MD
Underberg, James A., MD
Weber, Scott, MD

Weiner, David J., MD
Weiss, Nancy L., MD
Zachary, Kirk J., MD

Medical Oncology

Buckner, Jeffrey A., MD
Mernick, Mitchel, MD

Nephrology

Rodman, John S., MD

OB/GYN

Faroqui, Raufa, MD
Fischer, Ilene M., MD
Ho, Alison, MD
Hobgood, Laura S., MD
Selick, Caryn E., MD

Pediatrics

Schwartz, Stephen, MD

Pulmonology

Bregman, Zachary, MD
Schwartz, Lawrence P, MD

Rheumatolgy

Kramer, Sara, MD

MIDTOWN WEST DOCTORS

Gastroenterology

Altman, Kenneth A., MD
Attia, Albert, MD

Geriatrics

Babitz, Lisa E., MD
Kamlet, David A., MD

Hematology

Frankel, Etta B., MD

Internal Medicine

Altman, Kenneth A., MD
Attia, Albert, MD
Babitz, Lisa E., MD
Frankel, Etta B., MD
Kamlet, David A., MD
Young, Kevin S., MD

Medical Oncology

Frankel, Etta B., MD

UPPER EAST SIDE

Adolescent Medicine

Pegler, Cynthia, MD

Allergy & Immunology

Falk, George A., MD
Levine, Susan, MD
Lichtenfeld, Amy D., MD

Cardiology

Andersen, Holly S., MD
Ellis, George C., MD
Franklin, Kenneth W., MD
Graf, Jeffrey H., MD
Kennish, Arthur, MD
Mattes, Leonard, MD

Critical Care

Konecky, Alan, MD
Posner, David H., MD

Dermatology

Demar, Leon K., MD
Kling, Alan R., MD

Endocrinology

Bernstein, Gerald, MD
Merker, Edward, MD

Gastroenterology

Baiocco, Peter, MD
Cantor, Michael C., MD
Goldberg, Edward S., MD
Harris, Lucinda A., MD
Loria, Jeffrey M., MD
Present, Daniel H., MD
Weintraub, Gerald, MD
Yaffe, Bruce H., MD

Geriatrics

Schayes, Bernard, MD

Gynecology

Berman, Joan K., MD
Fishbane-Mayer, Jill, MD
Hirsch, Lissa, MD

Hematology

Beautyman, Elizabeth J.
Edwards, Colleen A., MD
Geltman, Richard L., MD
Lewin, Margaret, MD

Infectious Diseases

Fisher, Laura, MD
Hart, Catherine, MD
Levine, Susan, MD
Nash, Thomas W., MD

Internal Medicine

Abrams, Robert S., MD
Adler, Jack J., MD
Ament, Joseph D., MD
Andersen, Holly S., MD
Baiocco, Peter, MD
Bardes, Charles L., MD
Beautyman, Elizabeth J.
Belenkov, Elliot, MD
Bernstein, Gerald, MD
Bernstein, Stephen J., MD
Brandon, Donald E., MD

Cantor, Michael C., MD
Drapkin, Arnold, MD
Edwards, Colleen A., MD
Ellis, George C., MD
Falk, George A., MD
Fallick, Nina, MD
Fisher, Laura, MD
Franklin, Kenneth W., MD
Furman, Alice, MD
Geltman, Richard L., MD
Glick, Jeffrey, MD
Goldberg, Edward S., MD
Golden, Flavia A., MD
Graf, Jeffrey H., MD
Harris, Lucinda A., MD
Hart, Catherine, MD
Horbar, Gary, MD
Horovitz, H. Leonard, MD
Hurd, Beverly, MD
Keller, Raymond S., MD
Kennish, Arthur, MD
Klein, Susan, MD
Konecky, Alan, MD
Lamm, Steven, MD
Leventhal, Gerald H., MD
Levine, Susan, MD
Lewin, Margaret, MD
Lichtenfeld, Amy D., MD
Loria, Jeffrey M., MD
Mattes, Leonard, MD
Merker, Edward, MD
Moyer, Lawson, MD
Nash, Thomas W., MD
Nicolaides, Maria N., MD
Posner, David H., MD
Present, Daniel H, MD
Radin, Allen, MD
Rooney, Ellen, MD
Ruden, Ronald, MD
Schayes, Bernard, MD
Solomon, David Y., MD
Weinstein, Melvin, MD

Weintraub, Gerald, MD
Weiser, Frank M., MD
Yaffe, Bruce H., MD
Yanoff, Allen, MD

Medical Oncology
Belenkov, Elliot, MD
Geltman, Richard L., MD
Lewin, Margaret, MD

Nephrology
Nicolaides, Maria N., MD

OB/GYN
Adler, Alan A., MD
Bello, Gaetano, MD
Berman, Alvin, MD
Brodman, Michael, MD
Carlon, Anne, MD
Chin Quee, Karlene, MD
Corio, Laura, MD
Creatura, Chris, MD
Friedman, Lynn, MD
Goldman, Gary H., MD
Lebowitz, Nancy, MD
Livoti, Carol, MD
Manos, Ellen, MD
Nachamie, Rebecca, MD
Park, Brian, MD
Reiss, Ronald J., MD
Sassoon, Albert K., MD,
Sillay, Laila R., MD
Wenger, Judith, MD
Yale, Suzanne, MD
Zilberstein, Inga, MD

Pediatric Pulmonology
Elbirt-Bender, Paula, MD

Pediatrics
Daar, Eileen R., MD
Elbirt-Bender, Paula, MD
Goldstein, Judith, MD
Kessler, Ruth E., MD

Lantz, Howard, MD
Pasquariello, Palmo, MD
Pegler, Cynthia, MD
Popper, Laura, MD
Seed, Wm., MD
Skog, Donald R., MD
Smith, David I., MD
Snyder, Fredrick E., MD
Spielman, Gerald, MD
Stein, Barry B., MD
Weller, Alan S., MD
Wishnick, Marcia M., MD

Physical Medicine & Rehabilitation
Solomon, David Y., MD

Pulmonology
Abrams, Robert S., MD
Adler, Jack J., MD
Falk, George A., MD
Horovitz, H Leonard, MD
Keller, Raymond S., MD
Konecky, Alan, MD
Nash, Thomas W., MD
Posner, David H., MD

Rheumatolgy
Bernstein, Stephen J., MD
Leventhal, Gerald H., MD
Radin, Allen, MD

UPPER WEST SIDE

Endocrinology
Colt, Edward, MD

Family Practice
Aguero, Jose, MD
Bauchman, Gail, MD
Shepard, Richard, MD
Tamarin, Steven, MD

Gastroenterology

Arons, Elliot, MD

General Practice

Shapiro, Irene, MD

Geriatrics

Goodman, Karl, MD
Wiechowski, Michael, MD

Gynecology

Beitner, Orit, MD

Infectious Diseases

Fried, Richard P., MD
Silverman, David, MD

Internal Medicine

Amiraian, Richard H., MD
Arons, Elliot, MD
Baskin, David H., MD
Bendo, Dominick, MD
Blye, Ellen, MD
Charap, Peter, MD
Cohen, Albert, MD
Colt, Edward, MD
Diamond, Carol, MD
Fried, Richard P., MD
Goodman, Karl, MD
Kadet, Alan, MD

Larson, Carol, MD
Painter, Lucy N., MD
Silverman, David, MD
Sorra, Lembitu, MD
Suozzi, William, MD
Wiechowski, Michael, MD

Medical Oncology

Diamond, Carol, MD

Pediatric Allergy & Immunology

Lazarus, Herbert, MD

Pediatric Endocrinology

Rosenbaum, Michael, MD
Softness, Barney, MD

Pediatric Rheumatology

Lazarus, Herbert, MD

Pediatrics

Kahn, Max A., MD
Khanna, Kussum, MD
Lazarus, Herbert, MD
Rosenbaum, Michael, MD
Rosenfeld, Suzanne, MD
Softness, Barney, MD
Van Gilder, Max, MD

Medicaid Providers

Family Practice

Chung, Bruce, MD

Infectious Diseases

Montana, John, MD

Internal Medicine

Bruno, Peter, J., MD
Glick, Jeffrey, MD
Montana, John, MD
Solomon, David Y., MD

Physical Medicine & Rehabilitation

Solomon, David, Y., MD

Medicare Providers

Allergy & Immunology
Falk, George A., MD
Levine, Susan, MD
Lichtenfeld, Amy D., MD

Cardiology
Andersen, Holly S., MD
Graf, Jeffrey H., MD
Kennish, Arthur, MD
Mattes, Leonard, MD
Mueller, Richard L., MD

Critical Care Medicine
Bahr, Gerald S., MD
Konecky, Alan, MD
Posner, David H., MD

Dermatology
Demar, Leon K., MD
Kling, Alan R., MD
Scheiner, Avery M., MD

Emergency Medicine
Isaacs, Daryl M., MD

Endocrinology
Bernstein, Gerald, MD
Colt, Edward, MD
Merker, Edward, MD
Park, Constance, MD

Family Practice
Aguero, Jose, MD
Braun, James F., MD
Buchel, Tamara L., MD
Chung, Bruce, MD
Goldberg, Richard, MD
Horowitz, Mark E., MD
Leeds, Gary, MD
Leichman, Gerald, MD
Levy, Albert, MD
Olmscheid, Bruce, MD
Ravetz, Valerie, MD
Shepard Richard, MD
Tamarin Steven, MD

Gastroenterology
Arons, Elliot, MD
Attia, Albert, MD
Baiocco, Peter, MD
Bearnot, Robert, MD
Brettholz, Edward, MD
Goldberg, Edward S., MD
Loria, Jeffrey M., MD
Lustbader, Ian, MD
Pearlman, Kenneth I., MD
Present, Daniel H., MD
Weber, Scott, MD
Yaffe, Bruce H., MD
Zachary, Kirk J., MD

General Practice

Shapiro, Irene, MD

General Surgery

Cho, Sam K., MD

Geriatrics

Babitz, Lisa E., MD
Bernstein, Donald H., MD
Goodman, Karl, MD
Halper, Peter, MD
Levy, Albert, MD
Mernick, Mitchel, MD
Schayes, Bernard, MD
Wiechowski, Michael, MD

Gynecology

Fishbane-Mayer, Jill, MD

Hematology

Beautyman, Elizabeth J., MD
Buckner, Jeffrey A., MD
Edwards, Colleen A., MD
Frankel, Etta B., MD
Geltman, Richard L., MD
Lewin, Margaret, MD
Vizel-Schwartz, Monique, MD

Infectious Diseases

Bell, Evan T., MD
Fried, Richard P., MD
Gale, Robert K., MD
Hart, Catherine, MD
Levine, Susan, MD
Montana, John, MD
Rudin, Debra, MD
Silverman, David, MD
Wallach, Jeffrey, MD

Internal Medicine

Abrams, Robert S., MD
Adler, Jack J., MD
Adler, Mitchell A., MD

Ament, Joseph D., MD
Amiraian, Richard H., MD
Andersen, Holly S., MD
Arons, Elliot, MD
Attia, Albert, MD
Babitz, Lisa E., MD
Bahr, Gerald S., MD
Baiocco, Peter, MD
Bardes, Charles L., MD
Barnes, Edward, MD
Baskin, David H., MD
Bearnot, Robert, MD
Beautyman, Elizabeth J., MD
Belenkov, Elliot, MD
Bell, Evan T., MD
Bendo, Dominick, MD
Bernstein, Donald H., MD
Bernstein, Gerald, MD
Blye, Ellen, MD
Bregman, Zachary, MD
Brettholz, Edward, MD
Bruno, Peter J., MD
Buckner, Jeffrey A., MD
Charap, Peter, MD
Cohen, Albert, MD
Cohen, Robert L., MD
Colt, Edward, MD
Dhalla, Satish, MD
Diamond, Carol, MD
Edwards, Colleen A., MD
Falk, George A., MD
Fallick, Nina, MD
Frankel, Etta B., MD
Fried, Richard P., MD
Friedman, Jeffrey P., MD
Furman, Alice, MD
Gale, Robert K., MD
Geltman, Richard L., MD
Glick, Jeffrey, MD
Goldberg, Edward S., MD
Golden, Flavia A., MD
Goodman, Karl, MD
Graf, Jeffrey H., MD

Grossman, Howard A., MD
Halper, Peter, MD
Hammer, David, MD
Hart, Catherine, MD
Hauptman, Allen S., MD
Higgins, Lawrenc A.,DO,MPH
Hurd, Beverly, MD
Isaacs, Daryl M., MD
Kabakow, Bernard, MD
Kadet, Alan, MD
Kaufman, David L., MD
Keller, Raymond S., MD
Kennish, Arthur, MD
Klein, Susan, MD
Konecky, Alan, MD
Langelier, Carolyn A., MD
Levine, Susan, MD
Lewin, Margaret, MD
Lichtenfeld, Amy D., MD
Loria, Jeffrey M., MD
Lustbader, Ian, MD
Lutsky, Eric, MD
Mattes, Leonard, MD
Merker, Edward, MD
Mernick, Mitchel, MD
Montana, John, MD
Mueller, Richard L., MD
Nadel, Lester, MD
Nicolaides, Maria N., MD
Painter, Lucy N., MD
Palumbo, Michael J., MD
Park, Constance, MD
Pearlman, Kenneth I., MD
Perskin, Michael, MD
Pitaro, Gregory, MD
Posner, David H., MD
Present, Daniel H., MD
Ruden, Ronald, MD
Rudin, Debra, MD
Schayes, Bernard, MD
Schwartz, Lawrence P., MD
Shay, William E., MD
Silverman, David, MD

Solomon, David Y., MD
Sorra, Lembitu, MD
Strauss, Steven, MD
Suozzi, William, MD
Underberg, James A., MD
Vizel-Schwartz, Monique, MD
Wallach, Jeffrey, MD
Weber, Scott, MD
Weiner, David J., MD
Weinstein, Melvin, MD
Weiser, Frank M., MD
Weiss, Nancy L., MD
Wiechowski, Michael, MD
Woronoff, Richard S., MD
Yaffe, Bruce H., MD
Young, Kevin S., MD
Zachary, Kirk J., MD

Medical Oncology

Belenkov, Elliot, MD
Buckner, Jeffrey A., MD
Diamond, Carol, MD
Frankel, Etta B., MD
Geltman, Richard L., MD
Kabakow, Bernard, MD
Vizel-Schwartz, Monique, MD
Lewin, Margaret, MD
Mernick, Mitchel, MD

Nephrology

Nicolaides, Maria N., MD

OB/GYN

Bello, Gaetano, MD
Berman, Alvin, MD
Brodman, Michael, MD
Cavalli, Adele, MD
Corio, Laura, MD
Friedman, Lynn, MD
Gruss, Leslie, MD
Ho, Alison, MD
Hobgood, Laura S., MD
Reiss, Ronald J., MD

OB/GYN (cont'd)

Yale, Suzanne, MD
Zilberstein., Inga, MD

Physical Medicine
& Rehabilitation

Solomon, David Y., MD

Pulmonology

Abrams, Robert S., MD

Pulmonology

Adler, Jack J., MD
Bregman, Zachary, MD

Falk, George A., MD
Hammer, David, MD
Keller, Raymond S., MD
Konecky, Alan, MD
Posner, David H., MD
Schwartz, Lawrence P., MD
Woronoff, Richard S., MD

Rheumatolgy

Bernstein, Donald H., MD

Evenings Hours Index

Adolescent Medicine
Pegler, Cynthia, MD

Allergy & Immunology
Levine, Susan, MD

Cardiology
Mueller, Richard, L., MD

Dermatology
Kling, Alan R., MD
Scheiner, Avery M., MD

Emergency Medicine
Isaacs, Daryl M, MD

Endocrinology
Colt, Edward, MD
Merker, Edward, MD

Family Practice
Aguero, Jose, MD
Braun, James F., MD
Chung, Bruce, MD
Clements, Jerry, MD
Leichman, Gerald, MD
Ravetz, Valerie, MD
Tamarin, Steven, MD

Gastroenterology
Arons, Elliot, MD
Bearnot, Robert, MD
Brettholz, Edward, MD
Goldberg, Edward S., MD
Loria, Jeffrey M., MD
Lustbader, Ian, MD
Pearlman, Kenneth I., MD
Yaffe, Bruce H., MD

Geriatrics
Halper, Peter, MD
Kamlet, David A., MD
Mernick, Mitchel, MD

Gynecology
Beitner, Orit, MD

Hematology
Vizel-Schwartz, Monique, MD

Infectious Diseases
Gale, Robert K., MD
Levine, Susan, MD
Montana, John, MD
Rudin, Debra, MD
Silverman, David, MD
Wallach, Jeffrey, MD

Pediatrics

Lazarus, Herbert, MD
Coffey, Robert J., MD
Daar, Eileen R., MD
Elbirt-Bender, Paula, MD
Goldstein, Judith, MD
Grunfeld, Paul, MD
Kahn, Max A, MD
Khanna, Kussum, MD
Lantz, Howard, MD
Murphy, Ramon J. C., MD
Pegler, Cynthia, MD
Popper, Laura, MD

Rosenbaum, Michael, MD
Rosenfeld, Suzanne, MD
Skog, Donald R., MD
Softness, Barney, MD
Stein, Barry B., MD
Wishnick, Marcia M., MD

Pulmonology

Adler, Jack J., MD

Rheumatolgy

Bernstein, Stephen J., MD

Saturday Hours
Index

Cardiology

Mueller, Richard L., MD

Endocrinology

Colt, Edward, MD

Family Practice

Aguero, Jose, MD
Chung, Bruce, MD
Horowitz, Mark E., MD
Leichman, Gerald, MD
Levy, Albert, MD
Shepard, Richard, MD

Gastroenterology

Brettholz, Edward, MD

General Practice

Shapiro, Irene, MD

Geriatrics

Goodman, Karl, MD
Halper, Peter, MD
Levy, Albert, MD
Mernick, Mitchel, MD
Wiechowski, Michael, MD

Gynecology

Beitner, Orit, MD

Infectious Diseases

Gale, Robert K., MD

Internal Medicine

Amiraian, Richard H., MD
Beitler, Martin, MD
Bendo, Dominick, MD
Brettholz, Edward, MD
Colt, Edward, MD
Gale, Robert K., MD
Goodman, Karl, MD
Halper, Peter, MD
Hammer, David, MD
Mernick, Mitchel, MD
Mueller, Richard L., MD
Perskin, Michael, MD
Solomon, David Y., MD
Weiss, Nancy L., MD
Wiechowski, Michael, MD

Medical Oncology

Mernick, Mitchel, MD

OB/GYN

Bello, Gaetano, MD
Cavalli, Adele, MD
Hobgood, Laura S., MD
Nachamie, Rebecca, MD
Park, Brian, MD

Private Practitioners

PRIVATE PRACTICE

Adolescent Medicine
Pegler, Cynthia, MD

Cardiology
Ellis, George C., MD

Family Practice
Clements, Jerry, MD

Gastroenterology
Altman, Kenneth A., MD
Cantor, Michael C., MD
Present, Daniel H., MD

Gynecology
Beitner, Orit, MD
Berman, Joan K., MD
Fishbane-Mayer, Jill, MD
Hirsch, Lissa, MD

Infectious Diseases
Gale, Robert K., MD
Hart, Catherine, MD
Nash, Thomas W., MD
Silverman, David, MD

Internal Medicine
Altman, Kenneth A., MD
Cantor, Michael C., MD

Ellis, George C., MD
Gale, Robert K., MD
Hart, Catherine, MD
Higgins, Lawrence A., DO, MPH
Nash, Thomas W., MD
Present, Daniel H., MD
Rodman, John S., MD
Silverman, David, MD
Sorra, Lembitu, MD
Yanoff, Allen, MD

Nephrology
Rodman, John S., MD

OB/GYN
Bello, Gaetano, MD
Carlon, Anne, MD
Cavalli, Adele, MD
Chin Quee, Karlene, MD
Creatura, Chris, MD
Livoti, Carol, MD
Manos, Ellen, MD
Sassoon, Albert K., MD, MPH
Sillay, Laila R., MD
Wenger, Judith, MD
Yale, Suzanne, MD

Pediatric Endocrinology
Softness, Barney, MD

Pediatric Pulmonology
Elbirt-Bender, Paula, MD

Pediatrics

Elbirt-Bender, Paula, MD
Lantz, Howard, MD
Murphy, Ramon J, C., MD
Pegler, Cynthia, MD
Popper, Laura, MD
Seed, Wm., MD

Skog, Donald R., MD
Smith, David I., MD
Softness, Barney, MD
Stein, Barry B., MD

Pulmonology

Nash, Thomas W., MD

Hearing Impaired Services

Dermatology
Demar, Leon, K., MD

Emergency Medicine
Lewin, Neal A., MD

Endocrinology
Park, Constance, MD

Gastroenterology
Cantor, Michael C., MD

Geriatrics
Kamlet, David A., MD
Mernick, Mitchel, MD

Infectious Diseases
Montana, John, MD
Silverman, David, MD

Internal Medicine
Beitler, Martin, MD
Bruno, Peter J., MD
Cantor, Michael C., MD
Grossman, Howard A., MD

Kadet, Alan, MD
Kamlet, David A., MD
Lewin, Neal A., MD
Mernick, Mitchel, MD
Montana, John, MD
Nicolaides, Maria, N., MD
Park, Constance, MD
Shay, William E., MD
Silverman, David, MD
Strauss, Steven, MD

Medical Oncology
Mernick, Mitchel, MD

Nephrology
Nicolaides, Maria N., MD

OB/GYN
Bello, Gaetano, MD
Brodman, Michael, MD
Cavalli, Adele, MD
Chin Quee, Karlene, MD
Friedman, Lynn, MD
Nachamie, Rebecca, MD
Yale Suzanne, MD

Get $5 Off
Next Year's Book!

Take part in our survey!

Receive $5 off your pre-release copy of next year's Guide simply by taking part in our survey. Fill in your name and address below and we'll send you our survey. Return the completed survey to us and we'll send you a certificate, worth $5 off the price (when purchased directly from us) of the '99 edition of **The Manhattan Doctor Guide** and we'll notify when the book is ready to ship.

Name:

Address:

City, State and Zip:

Get Your Own!

Get your own copy of our Guide. Send this coupon along with your check for $14.95 per copy to us at the address below and we will speed your copy on its way.

Name: _____

Address: _____

City, State and Zip: _____

MAIL TO:

RadComm, Inc.
Box 717
New York, NY 10028